parenting made easy *The early years*

A bag of tricks approach to parenting the 1 to 5 year old

Dr Anna Cohen

First published 2015 by:
Australian Academic Press Group Pty. Ltd.
18 Victor Russell Drive
Samford Valley QLD 4520, Australia
www.australianacademicpress.com.au

Copyright © 2015 Anna Cohen

Copying for educational purposes
The *Australian Copyright Act 1968* (Cwlth) allows a maximum of one chapter or 10% of this book, whichever is the greater, to be reproduced and/or communicated by any educational institution for its educational purposes provided that the educational institution (or the body that administers it) has given a remuneration notice to Copyright Agency Limited (CAL) under the Act.
For details of the CAL licence for educational institutions contact:
Copyright Agency Limited, 19/157 Liverpool Street, Sydney, NSW 2000.
E-mail info@copyright.com.au

Production and communication for other purposes
Except as permitted under the Act, for example a fair dealing for the purposes of study, research, criticism or review, no part of this book may be reproduced, stored in a retrieval system, or transmitted in any form or by any means electronic, mechanical, photocopying, recording or otherwise without prior written permission of the copyright holder.

Parenting Made Easy: The Early Years

ISBN   9781922117441 (paperback)
ISBN   9781922117458 (ebook)

Publisher & Copy Editor: Stephen May

Cover design: Maria Biaggini, The Letter Tree

Page design & typesetting: Australian Academic Press

Printing: Lightning Source

For my niece
Harlia
who is truly in the wondrous early years
To my Godson
Jagger
who is moving into the preschool years
And my daughters
who have taught me so much about this precious time

Acknowledgements

I would like to thank my family for their continued support and for putting up with my enthusiasm for writing and the disruption it causes in our busy lives and home. I am grateful to my two precious, wilful, empathetic daughters; your pride in what I do makes it all so worthwhile. To my husband AP, all I can say is thank you, without your care this would not be possible. I am also so thankful to my mother and wonderful girlfriends, Elle Levey, Emma Caldwell, Kelly Hammond, Marina J and Tash Rumble for all the listening that they do. Lastly, I am indebted to my amazing, dedicated and passionate colleagues who I am so privileged to work with and with whom I hope to continue to work for many more years.

Contents

Acknowledgements iv
Introduction vii

Chapter 1: Development 1

The early years 1
Birth to five years 2
Characteristics of the child during the early years 6
Building your bag of tricks 11

**Chapter 2: Attunement and the
 development of strong relationships 15**

Attuned parenting 15
Mindful parenting 18
Simple mindfulness strategy 18
The brain 19
Building your bag of tricks 22

Chapter 3: Raising emotionally intelligent children 25

Window of tolerance 27
Cultivating emotional intelligence 29
Affirming messages during the early years 30
Building your bag of tricks 31
Development and affirming messages 32

**Chapter 4: Responding to your child's
 developmental needs 39**

Commonly misunderstood behaviours 43
Encouraging desirable behaviour 47
Child-centred time 48
Building your bag of tricks 49

**Chapter 5: Acknowledging desirable
 behaviour and reflecting feelings 53**

Effective acknowledgement 53
Ways to acknowledge 54

Proximity 56
Attachment rich and attachment neutral engagement 57
Be consistent 59
Reflecting feelings 59
Building your bag of tricks 61

Chapter 6: Giving effective instructions and choices 65

The typical escalation trap 66
Typical requests made 66
How to stop the escalation trap 67
Simple steps for effective instruction giving 69
Terminating instructions 70
The in-charge parent 72
Using choices with your child 74
How to make instructions effective 75
Building your bag of tricks 75

Chapter 7: Managing parenting challenges 77

Consequences 77
Avoiding arguments 78
Reduce negative emotional expression 78
Planned ignoring 79
Logical consequences 80
Quiet time 82
Cool down 84
Post-incident discussion 86
Managing high-risk situations 87
Calming strategies 89
Building your bag of tricks 90

Chapter 8: Pulling it all together — your bag of tricks 95

Tips for encouraging considerate behaviour 95
Tips for discouraging inconsiderate behaviour 97
Parenting tips 101

References 105

Introduction

For children the early years are a time of innocence and joy. Yet for their parents and other caregiving adults it is often a tricky and challenging time — a time when you will watch your baby fade and a child emerge, a time of amazing growth, development and change. With each developmental stage new challenges need to be faced and solved. Responding to your child's needs is not about rescuing them when they are upset, but rather providing consistent care, protection and emotional support. Such authoritative parenting is characterised by firm, warm, expectations with clear limit setting while encouraging independent thinking and displaying unconditional love. All children regardless of their age and stage need to feel a sense of dignity and competency. Our job as parents and responsible caregivers is to encourage the greatness of our children and to raise well-adjusted, confident, compassionate, considerate individuals.

Throughout this book I will use the terms parent and parenting as inclusive of all parent/caregiver relationships.

The early years are a time of rapid development. By understanding how children develop, we can have fair expectations of them and can empathise and find effective strategies and tools to teach and nurture them through each psychological stage successfully. Through our empathy, humour, good judgment, compassion and ability to regulate our emotions we help our children to be securely attached and support the development of their brain. By understanding the development of children in the early years we are better able to find solutions to the characteristic problems that occur at this time.

As a parent or caregiver of a child in the early years your 'bag of tricks' must take into account your child's development and cognitive (thinking) abilities at any given stage. People progress through stages of emotional development during a lifetime. Understanding this helps us become more aware of ourselves emotionally as parents and caregivers. It also provides us with an insightful perspective on others that helps us to treat children with empathy and compassion. Learning how children develop emotionally and socially helps parents and other caregiving adults to set realistic and fair expectations of children as they move towards the middle (school) years.

The parenting approach advocated in this book stems from the notion that children by virtue of being children will make behavioural errors and that it is the job of parents and responsible caregivers to love and believe in them and to model and teach respectful communication. In raising well-adjusted and confident children it is essential that we share our preschooler's enthusiasm for life and that the parenting practices employed teach rather than punish or shame. This authoritative approach is one that supports children in meeting their developmental tasks, promotes respectful interactions, does not suggest that the child is wrong or bad and sets them up for success not failure.

The information contained in these pages is designed to be a 'bag of tricks' for you to use with kindness in your parenting to foster your child's positive self-identity. These strategies promote opportunities for positive interactions and assist in the building of supportive parent–child relationships. The strategies advocated promote positive nurturing relationships while equipping parents with skills to manage problematic behaviour. The behaviour management approaches are not intended to be the magic solution to all your difficulties and may need to be changed slightly to suit your family or your own way of speaking. The ideas in this book have worked for thousands of families, but they are examples and suggestions only. Remember, you're the one who knows your family inside out and that by being clear in your expectations, trusting your capability, celebrating your resourcefulness and being open to finding effective solutions to parenting challenges you can be the sort of parent you want to be.

Chapter 1

Development

The early years

The early relationship that you develop with your child is crucial for their brain development and emotional regulation. Children's brains develop more quickly from birth to five than at any other point in their lifetime. Infants and young children's brains are hardwired to learn even before they are born. In these early years they are constantly learning from everything that happens around them. They are sensitive to the emotional atmosphere in their family and learn their social skills from the experiences they have with their parents, caregivers and by playing with other children. The more positive experiences a child has, the more their brain will develop.

Children's character develops over time. Character development can be influenced by how parents teach children to respect themselves, other people and all living things. The values of peaceful problem solving, honesty and compassion are learnt and are greatly influenced by what parents and other caregivers model. Children in the early years imitate the responses they see in the significant people who surround them. Because of this, family life is central to emotional learning.

By understanding how children learn and grow, we can be mindful in our parenting and establish fair and reasonable expectations. We can also develop effective strategies and tools to teach and nurture successfully. Although no two children grow and develop at the same rate it is generally agreed that there are normal signs of development.

Birth to five years

Satisfaction with who we are and how we are loved is an essential part of a happy and fulfilling family life and the foundation from which optimal child development flows. Babies from birth to the age of one are dependent on their parents or caregivers for having their needs met and for learning to interact with the world around them. With consistent and attuned parenting infants are able to meet their developmental trajectory. For example, positive gazes and talking to a baby stimulates pleasurable feelings, which in turn assist in brain development and provide the template for future healthy relationships.

During the first two to three years of life, the emotional centres of a child's brain are developing faster than their talking, thinking and reasoning centres. Because of this different rate of development in the feeling and thinking centres of the brain children in the early years can get very emotional and are not capable of planning and reasoning. Infants are not able to talk about how they feel or to calm themselves down. Toddlers and young children live in an emotional world and essentially 'act without thinking'.

Children's emotional patterns develop early in the infancy stage. Attuned parents enhance the baby's ability to learn to cope with strong feelings and allow the infant to regulate *negative affect* (strong negative emotions). When the infant's needs are met they are able to develop a sense of trust in the world as predictable and safe. A sense of optimism develops in children who emerge from the first year of life with a favourable balance of trust over mistrust.

An important foundation for infant development is the maintenance of a routine, which helps to scaffold everyday life as the baby grows through childhood and develops into their adult self. Routines and rituals help children to understand sequence, time, and to learn about expected and considerate behaviour.

The tremendous growth that happens for an infant as they develop from a baby to a toddler is a busy time. One of the major developmental tasks in this period is to explore and learn to trust their environment. Children during this stage (nearing one year) are active and curious and they begin to want some time and space away from others to develop their separateness and autonomy. The important task of being able to separate from parents is the start of children becoming independent. As parents and responsible adults it is important to provide the structure to the preschool-aged child's environment to thus give them the freedom to grow. Toddlers require their parents help to regulate (manage) their emotions. They frequently need to be 'down-regulated' from a naturally high emotional state, which results from all their exploring and busy movement, to a calm state.

Toddlers' brains grow rapidly with the most growth occurring in the feeling, emotional centre of the brain as well as in the areas that relate to physical skills such as walking, running, jumping, balancing and feeding themselves. Skill mastery requires that they practice a particular skill over and over again. Toddlers feel good about themselves and love the sense of power they get from being able to do things on their own. Identity formation starts to occur at eighteen months of age and toddlers start to develop a sense of self — 'me' and 'mine'. Due to having active emotion centres in the brain, toddlers react emotionally when frustrated. After eighteen months of age the centres of the brain that help to regulate and control impulses start to develop.

There is also a major developmental shift in the early years. Babies see themselves as an extension of their mother or caregiver, while toddlers (aged one to two years of age) progressively come to see themselves as separate from their mother or caregiver and indeed as autonomous and having their own will. As the exploring toddler becomes aware of being separate from their parents, anxiety and fearfulness develop. An emerging sense of self occurs as the toddler oscillates between wanting to be independent and dependent at the same time. This apparent ambivalence leads to anger outbursts, which are frequently directed towards the mother. During such tumultuous times, fathers and other significant adults need to be actively involved in helping the toddler to regulate their intense emotions.

As children grow into the preschool years (three to five years of age) the baby fades and the child emerges and they become increasingly confident in their abilities. There is a significant increase in physical competence and language skills. Children gain the ability to express both positive and negative feeling states with words. During these early years children crave knowledge, they seek to explore their environment and make sense of their world by asking many questions. The first steps towards autonomy are taken as children in the preschool years start to develop their identity and exercise power. During this goal-orientated period of development they show initiative and purpose in their play and are interesting, engaging and wonderful little people.

The imaginary play of the three to six-year-old is characterised by themes of power: heroes, battles and monsters emerge. Preschool-aged children like to feel powerful, and this is frequently played out in their imaginary play. Play is a way of experimenting with new roles and distinguishing what is real and what is imagined. Preschool-age children can oscillate between an awareness of what is real and what is make-believe. At one moment they may engage in elaborate imaginative play while at the next become terrified of a dress-up outfit or a scary character on television or in a book.

Words are significant and help children in the early years to feel important. The three-year-old child asks many 'why' questions. The four-year-old child has strong opinions and will often voice their displeasure such as, 'I don't like that, it is silly'. The five-year-old child is inquisitive, frequently wanting to find out how things work. Due to preschoolers learning that words have power, baby-talk, arguing, whining, whingeing and bad language may all surface during this developmental period.

Peers and the establishment of friendships are both important during the preschool years and many children will create imaginary friends. Despite being important, social interactions can often be tricky for children at this age and may be characterised by both pro-social and inconsiderate behaviour. During this developmental stage it is not uncommon for caring, imaginative, happy, tender moments to be present as well as periods of difficulty sharing and conflict in play.

As higher levels of socialisation emerge children may go through stages of hitting or grabbing to get what they need, followed by verbal aggression and even bribery ('if you give it to me, you can be my friend'). This awkward handling of social situations often requires adult input in order to help preschool-age children develop pro-social behaviour and manage conflict with their peers. During the preschool years children typically break rules and can be challenging in their behaviour. Such behaviour is developmentally normal and is the first step towards acquiring an internalised ethic and individuality. Observing rules and expectations along with the making of rules both become important developmental tasks as children move into the middle years (six to twelve years) and are learnt as children progress through the early years.

Characteristics of the child during the early years

Job of the one to five-year-old child

- they learn to feel good about who they are
- they get to know the world — people, animals and nature
- they begin to understand that everything they do has consequences — good and bad
- they learn through repetition
- they start to learn how to get along with others in group situations
- they develop confidence in themselves and try new things
- they start to identify the difference between make-believe and reality
- they start to develop a sense of humour
- they learn that not everything works the way they want it to
- they soak up knowledge from everything they touch, smell, hear and taste

Typical behaviours of the one to five-year-old child

- they tend to view the world in terms of their own wants and needs
- they are curious
- they play make-believe games (mums, dads, builders, doctors)
- they ask a lot of questions ('why?' 'how?')
- they start to play games that have rules
- they begin to play with others
- they begin to ask for things they want

- they do things to see how you will react
- they develop frustration and fear due to the developmental need to exercise autonomy and separateness

Specific skills of the one to five-year-old child
Aged twelve to eighteen months

- they are curious, enthusiastic explorers
- they are constantly on the move
- they learn by doing
- they use one word to express whole thoughts ('walk' means 'I want to walk to the park')
- they are competent
- they are generally affectionate
- they can find simple solutions to many of their problems
- they understand more than they can express
- they imitate what you do
- they cannot anticipate consequences
- they cannot decide what is right or wrong
- they like to play alongside other children
- they can stack blocks, pull things and fill containers
- they begin to resist day-time sleeps
- they begin to show anger when they can't get their own way
- they often get upset when having their hair washed
- they are not ready to be toilet trained

Aged eighteen months to two years

- they test limits
- their vocabulary expands to using two to three word sentences
- their language takes on a commanding quality — 'more toast'

- they practice saying no and will say 'no', 'mine', 'me do', or other equivalents frequently
- they are picky eaters and are often disinterested in food
- their appetites vary
- they spill things a lot
- they frequently refuse to cooperate with usual routines such as sitting in their car seat, having a bath and going to bed
- they are often angry and try out many ways to show this
- they have tantrums
- they are fussy
- they whine and scream and will continue to demonstrate these behaviours for a long time if adults reinforce these responses
- they can be aggressive towards others with behaviours such as biting, hitting and snatching
- they have trouble sharing
- they oscillate between independence to dependence
- their language development is varied, some talk a lot while others do not
- they understand more words then they can say
- they understand simple instructions ('get your shoes') but get lost if asked to do more than two things at a time
- they can run but have a hard time stopping
- their fine motor abilities are varied — some can handle small objects well while others cannot
- they become more confident in their gross motor abilities and love to climb
- they like to put small objects into little holes such as their nose and ears
- they are literal and concrete in their understanding
- they learn through imitation

- they have a hard time sharing
- their memory is developing and they like stories and songs to be repeated

Aged three to five years
- they grow rapidly
- they use full sentences
- they are social within the family
- they are inquisitive and ask endless questions
- they can dress themselves
- they have good imaginations
- they have less frequent tantrums
- they can be aggressive towards others such as hitting and snatching
- they whinge and whine when tired
- they may wet the bed
- they may have night-time fears
- they are rule bound and tell tales when rules are broken by others
- they tend to be reactive and emotional
- they can have bad manners
- they may lie to avoid getting into trouble
- when they are angry they use mean words — 'I hate you', 'you are stupid', 'I am going to find a new family'
- they like to participate in jobs around the house
- they love to dress up (princesses, ballerinas, Spiderman and other superheroes)
- they enjoy playing with other children
- they can have imaginary friends

Helpful parent behaviour

- Love and enjoy them, help them when they need it.
- Affirm them when they meet their developmental tasks.
- Be reliable and trustworthy.
- Make their world predictable and consistent.
- Spend time with them.
- Respond to their needs.
- Help them to manage their feelings and settle their bodies.
- Understand that infants and toddlers have limited control over their emotional responses.
- Direct their behaviour.
- Teach them what they should be doing rather than controlling or entering into power struggles.
- Offer choices such as what clothes to wear or plate to use.
- Try to answer their questions as best you can.
- Avoid asking questions where there is no choice such as: 'say goodbye, thank you', rather than, 'can you say goodbye?'.
- Phrase statements in the positive such as: 'Keep your hands to yourself.' instead of: 'Don't hit!'.
- Help them to show how they are feeling.
- Accept both positive and negative feelings.
- Tell them when they do things right.
- Set clear, simple expectations — don't give in on everything.
- Protect them from people who upset them (i.e. tease or laugh at them).
- Teach them the correct names for body parts and what good and bad touch is.
- Teach them to say 'no' and to respect theirs' and other peoples' bodies.

- Let them experiment with pretend games.
- Let them try to do things by themselves.
- Pick your battles.
- Talk, read and sing to them.
- Say less and do more. For example, instead of telling them to go and brush their teeth, get up and take their hand and guide them; instead of nagging them to stop throwing their food or stop spilling their drink, show them how to do it.
- Model respectful communication and how to resolve conflict without physical or verbal attacks.
- Use caring non-sexual touch.

Building your bag of tricks

Children from birth to the age of five master a range of competencies. Toddlers require parents to help regulate their intense emotions while keeping up with their natural curiosity. When traversed well the toddler phase gives way to a preschool phase, where the child starts developing the ability to regulate their own emotions. Children in the early years can experience frustration and fear because they want to exercise their autonomy and thus this is a time that often requires limit setting by parents. Parenting practices employed during the early years set the scene and lay the foundation for all future parenting. As parents, there are many things that we can do to assist our children as they develop.

Toddlers (one to two years)

Infants and toddlers live in an emotional world. During this period of development infants rely on their parents to regulate their emotions and bring them back into a balanced emotional state. As an infant moves into the toddler phase tasks requiring balance and hand-eye coordination begin to emerge.

This practising period is a time where the infant moves more away from their parents and begins to individuate and separate. Visual referencing is used as the infant looks at their parent for safety and reassurance. The one-year-old loves movement and it is important to encourage them in seeking a level of independence. However, toddlers regularly need assistance in emotional regulation. During this time parents can help down-regulate high arousal and up-regulate low arousal in their child by labelling feelings and emotions, thus helping toddlers to feel safe and secure.

BAG OF TRICKS

1. **Be consistent and firm during limit testing moments.**
   Issue clear calm instructions and give affirming messages – 'I love you too much to let you out of your car seat. I want you safe.'

2. **Give choices.**
   Only give choices in situations when there are choices available.

3. **Have special toys available for high-risk times.**
   For example, use special books and toys while in the car seat or have a special dress up hat to wear in the car.

4. **Use one step requests or redirection.**
   Examples include: playing peek-a-boo, singing songs, playing imitation games (for example, tap a body part and then ask the child to copy the action, continue naming and touching parts of the body). Redirection is relational and works due to the secure relationship that has already been established.

5. **Be clear on the things you need to say 'no' about.**
   Be aware that children at this stage are developmentally practising saying 'no'. Acknowledge and affirm this developmental task and reflect that you are glad that your child is learning to say 'no'.

Preschoolers (two to five years)

As toddlers move into the preschool phase they show signs of self-regulation and begin to be able to inhibit their own behaviour. Expectations and limits provide structure for the preschool-aged child's environment and give them the freedom to grow.

BAG OF TRICKS

1. **Help toddlers and preschoolers to see the next step by announcing transitions before they occur.**
   Share something interesting that will be happening to help move the child along to the next step and reduce the likelihood of dysregulation.

2. **Communicate simple reasons.**
   For example, explain why play needs to stop using a matter-of-fact tone – 'I know you want to keep playing, but it is time to go home. Would you like your teddy bear?'

3. **Reflect the child's feelings to them.**
   'I know you want to keep playing but mummy has to get the dinner ready. Let's see how quickly we can pack the cars away.' 'I know you're frustrated that the crayon broke, but we don't throw crayons – let's see if we make it work.' 'That was scary wasn't it. You're okay.'

4. **Accept the child's emotions without feeling hurt.**
   'I know you're angry with mummy because you don't want to leave, but now we need to… Lets…'

5. **Keep the attachment bond present by using 'we'.**
   For example, 'We keep our hands and feet to ourselves.' 'We' refers to the parent-child relationship and helps the child to feel secure.

6. **Remember that children are still developing.**
   Don't forget that toddlers' and preschoolers' brains may resemble those of adults, but they do not yet function in the same way.

7. **Label the child's emotions.**
   Help them understand what they are feeling and to help name their feelings. Children feel secure when parents help them to up-regulate and down-regulate emotions. Children's emotions can be confronting and also dysregulating, triggering a parent's emotions. Using a calm matter-of-fact voice helps everyone move through difficult emotional states and is reregulating.

8. **Encourage problem solving by giving choices.**
   'Do you want to wear your pink socks today, or your purple ones?'

9. **Avoid questions when there is actually no choice.**
   For example, use 'Come here, thank you,' rather than, 'Can you come here?'

10. **Use positive statements.**
    'Come here Sam' or 'Use your spoon.'

11. **Try to understand their world.**
    Imagine the 'one world' view (centre of the universe) of toddlers and preschool-aged children.

Chapter 2

Attunement and the Development of Strong Relationships

There are many factors that influence the healthy development of children in the early years. Children's personality development is influenced by genetics, physical health, temperament and experiences. It is also shaped by the relationships they have with their parents. This is often referred to as the *attachment relationship*.

The attachment relationship is essential to the success of children's social and emotional development. Strong attachment bonds between a child and their parent is intricately linked to the child's emotion regulation (how they manage their emotions). How emotionally regulated the child is determines the health of their brain development (Schore, 2003). Helping a child to regulate their internal physiology allows them to use their whole brain. As parents and caregivers we can help a child to regulate their emotions through the attunement we give.

Attuned parenting

Attunement, as described by psychiatrist Daniel Stern (1985), is the intersubjective sharing of affect, which is essentially the process whereby the emotional state of one person is reflected in that of the other. Attunement between a parent and infant is an interaction in which the parent regulates the *affective* (emotional) states as they emerge from within the child. Such interactions serve to regulate the child as the parent's attuned response matches the affect state of the child. Attuned parents are able to respond when their infant becomes *dysregulated* by matching the child's affect and guiding the child into a *regulated state.*

Attuned parenting teaches a child that they can rely on their parent to help them when needed. Children of attuned parents intrinsically know that their parent is there to protect them and to help them regulate their emotions, at least until they are able to self-regulate. Relationship security leads to strong reflective functioning skills, (the awareness of one's own thoughts, feelings and intentions) and an ability to make sense of theirs' and others' behaviour. This attachment relationship forms the scaffolding from which a child's emotional intelligence, self-esteem, resilience, cognitive abilities and social skills develop.

Attuned parents respond sensitively to their child's needs enabling the child to explore their world. If the child's attachment system is activated, the parent is able to deactivate it by utilising their relationship with their child, allowing the child to regain emotional equilibrium and move on towards independence. In the course of this secure relationship the child learns through their interactions how to regulate their emotions. With time and further development children eventually learn to self-regulate their emotions. More specifically, they learn to auto-regulate.

Attuned parenting teaches children that they can:
- have their needs met,
- explore the world — because their parents are available when required,

- be successful, because they have been successful in having their needs met,
- engage in reciprocity, because they have learned it from their parents,
- make sense of their own and others' behaviour,
- notice and make sense of others' non-verbal expressions,
- be empathic,
- self-regulate their emotions, and
- have future successful relationships because they have already experienced these.

Children can learn and do all of the above because they understand that their parents are available when required, model reciprocity and trusting interactions, and demonstrate success in getting needs met. Children of attuned parents know they are worthy of positive, trusting interactions for they have had these from parents. They learn they are competent, lovable and capable individuals.

Nature is forgiving. We do not have to be perfect parents. There will always be times when parent–child interactions are less than perfect. Effective parenting is about being able to rectify disconnections and engage in relationship repair with our children. By repairing disconnections children learn that it is okay to make a mistake and to say 'sorry'. The key here is to be a *good enough* parent not a *perfect* parent. Disconnections which are repaired help babies, toddlers and young children to tolerate distress and assists in the development of healthy coping responses. Secure attachment is essential to children's healthy development into their adolescent and adult selves and is one area that we as parents and caregivers can influence.

Mindful parenting

Mindfulness or mindful awareness is defined by Kabat-Zinn (1994) as the awareness that emerges through paying attention on purpose, in the present moment and non-judgmentally, to the unfolding of experience from moment to moment. Mindful parenting is being present for your children. It means not having your attention turned away from what is happening between the two of you at that moment in time. It is an approach to parenting in which we are aware of our own thoughts and feelings while also being open to those of our children. When we are mindful as parents we enable our children to be fully present in the moment. The way we as parents communicate with our children determines how they experience themselves in that moment and influences the security of their attachment.

Mindful parents have intention in their actions. When we are mindful we intentionally choose how we will respond in that moment in time to a child's behaviour. Mindfulness supports parents in their efforts to develop thoughtful and contingent responses to their children. Parents who are mindful are able to be present during connecting interactions with their children and are less likely to be reactive in their responses. Connecting interactions such as talking, singing, cuddling, reading and playing with children help to grow their brains and strengthen relationships. Research has shown that when parents or caregivers relate to children with mindfulness they are able to think and act more rationally, experience less parenting stress and can be more present for their children's needs.

Simple mindfulness strategy

Relating to children with mindful awareness activates the area of the brain (the medial pre-frontal cortex) which deactivates defensive systems and allows for more rational thought. This allows parents to step outside of their own experience and be present to their child's needs.

The following is a simple mindfulness strategy that when practised regularly will help you to calm yourself quickly before managing any parenting challenges presented.

Stop, Breathe, Respond

Stop

- Stop what you are doing.
- Stand with your feet firmly on the floor and your body tall and straight.

Breathe

- Focus on your breath.
- Take a slow deep breath and notice the air go into your belly, then exhale slowly.
- Take three to five slow breaths.
- Focus your awareness on each in and out breath.
- Smile and stand for a moment longer.
- Ask yourself what you or your child needs right at this moment in time.

Respond

- Respond to your child with new insight and understanding.

The brain

The brain is a complex organ and undergoes rapid development during the early years. In fact children's brains develop more in the period from birth to five than they ever will again. Infants and young children's brains are sensitive to early experiences and change in response to their lived experience.

Therefore, early experiences and the environment in which children live both have a significant impact on the development of their brain. The more positive experiences a child has the more their brain develops. If a child has positive experiences early in life, it makes it easier for them to learn later on and is critical in shaping the structure of their brain. By knowing about a child's developing brain parents are better able to understand how children think, feel and behave and are thus more prepared to respond with appropriate and mindful practices.

Experiences influence the way children see themselves, their environment, their parents and others, as well as their emotional responses. The brain is designed to internally process information from the world and to generate a specific reaction. It is responsible for receiving and interpreting signals about experiences and storing memories that can be retrieved at a later date, thus shaping the future perception of experiences.

The brain is comprised of many different parts that do different things. These adapt to new experiences and learning. The left and the right sides of the brain differ significantly in the processing of incoming information. These two distinct areas of the brain are connected by bands of neural tissue which allow each side to function distinctly and to a certain degree independently. The organisation and number of neural connections influence how children understand their relationships, make sense of their experiences, learn and remember.

The unique and different processing of the right and left sides of the brain are essentially verbal and non-verbal. The left hemisphere of the brain processes information in a logical, linear fashion and is responsible for language-based processing. The right hemisphere processes the emotional, non-verbal content of experience.

Chapter 2 Attunement and the Development of Strong Relationships

The development of the right and left hemispheres occurs at different times over the course of a child's development. Children are right hemisphere dominant until about three years of age and as such, require primarily non-verbal communication with their parents. Higher levels of functioning occur when neural information passes between the hemispheres. As the two hemispheres become linked children become more able to put words to their feelings. This higher level of integrated functioning occurs as children develop into their adult selves and remains quite immature in the early years.

Like the right and left sides of the brain the upstairs (*cortex*) and downstairs (*limbic system*) parts of the brain are also quite different. The cortex is responsible for thinking and the limbic system is the emotional centre of the brain. During the toddler years the limbic system goes through rapid development and is dominant in the lives of children up to around four years of life. Due to the faster development of the limbic system, children in the early years have frequent tantrums and demonstrate irrational behaviours because they view the world through an emotional lens.

The last part of the brain to develop is the cortex. The cortex is the thinking part of the brain and is responsible for planning and reasoning. As the cortex develops children become able to think before they act. Development of the cortex is necessary for children to be able to self-regulate when experiencing strong emotion.

The limbic system and cortex are both susceptible to change as a result of a child's experience and the environment in which they live. With time and much repetition of similar experiences infants and young children's brains develop strong templates or blueprints. That is, the different areas of their brain become connected and integrated. Templates are formed in children's brains through repeated positive experiences in relationships with others as well as between themselves and the world. Such templates lead to strong beliefs about themselves as individuals, their safety, their lovableness, and their concept of relationships as fun and nurturing.

Children's emotional states are regulated through their relationships with their parent or caregiver. It is within the context of loving, warm relationships that children learn to trust, to feel safe to explore their world, and to develop a sense of identity and self-esteem. The primary attachment relationship between a child and parent shapes all future relationships and is the key to healthy brain development. Children's brains develop as a result of their relationship with other human brains — when children interact with people who love them their brains grow.

Building your bag of tricks

A child's personality is not only shaped by their temperament and genetics but also by their physical health and experiences. How we communicate with our children has a profound impact on their development. The ability to be sensitive and reciprocal in our communication is the foundation upon which secure attachment is built and is a cornerstone in a child's sense of safety and wellbeing. Early attachment relationships impact on the development of social skills, resilience, emotional intelligence, self-esteem and cognitive abilities.

You need to be aware of the following when building your bag of tricks:

- The practice of mindfulness allows parents to pay attention to what is happening within themselves.
- Mindfulness improves communication and relationships between parents and children.

- With regular mindfulness practice parents are more able to be connected with and attuned to their children's needs.
- Attunement is a parent's ability to understand and respond to their child's inner feeling world while encouraging mastery of the external world.
- Parent sensitivity, not temperament, impacts on the quality of a child's attachment.
- The ability to self-reflect as a parent is one of the more important elements associated with secure attachment.
- Young children have limited ability to be reasoned with and to link their thoughts, feelings and behaviours as the parts of the brain responsible for higher order thinking are not yet developed.
- During the early years children are operating from the emotional centre of the brain and can be challenging for parents when they exhibit emotional behaviour.
- Toddlers and young children need adults to help them to manage their strong feelings — their brains are immature and those under three years can generally not tell you what is wrong, thus they need parents and caregiving adults to help them feel safe.
- Due to the emotional centre of the brain developing before the thinking part children in the early years feel then act, instead of think then act.

BAG OF TRICKS

1. **Parent–child relationships influence the growth of children's brains.**
   Positive parent child relationships form the foundation for social and emotional success and development — emotional regulation is influenced through the quality of the parent-child relationship.

2. **Practice parent attunement.**
   Parent attunement supports the parent child relationship and teaches the child that they can be helped to regulate their emotions. With time, parent attunement facilitates the development of independence with emotion regulation and self-esteem.

3. **Be a mindful parent.**
   Mindful parents are able to be present during connecting interactions with their children and are less likely to be reactive in their responses. Remember to talk, sing, cuddle, read and play with your children – you will literally help to grow their brain!

4. **Remember a simple mindfulness strategy.**
   Remember the simple mindfulness strategy of stop, breathe, respond will help you to manage any parenting challenge presented.

5. **Good enough parenting is the key.**
   There is no such thing as perfect parenting. The essential ingredient in raising healthy well-adjusted children is mindful parenting, the ability to rectify disconnections and engage in relationship repair with our children.

Chapter 3

Raising Emotionally Intelligent Children

Emotions impact on every facet of life from creativity and achievement to relationships and productivity. The ability to handle strong feelings develops over time and impacts on a child's ability to cope and manage the problems that they face. Family life is important in the development of emotional learning. Shared experiences form the foundation on which relationships with children develop. Flexible mindful responding and being involved in children's emotional learning is crucial in parenting and in the development of *emotional intelligence.*

Emotional intelligence is the ability to recognise and control one's own emotions as well as to read and respond to the emotions of others. All infants are born with the capacity for emotional intelligence and the development of this in the early years is dependent on the relationships they have with their parents and significant caregivers. It is important that parents are aware of what is happening in their own brains and how they can regulate their reactions to their child's behaviour in order to remain attuned to their child.

When parents are tired, stressed, anxious or emotionally upset it is more difficult to be attuned to the emotional needs of children. At times of stress and distress the connections of the cortex, the thinking part of the brain, are blocked. When the cortex is blocked the limbic system is in full swing and a parent is more likely to act without thinking, to say and do things that they later regret. Such defensive systems can be switched off when a parent becomes mindful. Mindfulness activates the medial prefrontal cortex which allows for thinking and rational thought to occur. By developing mindfulness parents are more able to be present to their child's needs and foster emotional intelligence.

Emotional intelligence is as important as a child's cognitive ability for success at preschool, school and in the wider world. The emotional abilities that children develop during the early years form the foundation for all future learning. Confident and optimistic children do well at school and are resilient as they develop into their adult selves. Children who have parents that nurture their emotional intelligence through positive, authoritative, mindful, assertive parenting have a solid foundation from which to develop into happy, responsible and resilient adults.

Parents who are aware of their children's feelings are able to act as emotional coaches and teach them to understand emotions. When a child has a vocabulary with which to express their feelings they can better understand themselves and others. Such children are able to be resilient, to manage strong emotions and to control their anger. Children with a well-developed emotional intelligence acquire empathy and are able to read other people's feelings through their body language, tone of voice and facial expressions. Parents who model emotional intelligence to their children are more able to manage life's ups and downs and embrace their child's displays of anger, sadness, fear and other strong emotions. Emotional intelligence is enhanced when parents are able to be flexible and remain regulated during difficult parenting moments.

Window of tolerance

The parent–child relationship is complex. It is our job as parents to help children develop emotional intelligence and a spacious *window of tolerance*. A window of tolerance is a child's ability to think and feel at the same time. This starts to develop in the early years and continues throughout childhood.

Like our children, we also have a window of tolerance. However, the complex dynamics of the parent–child relationship often impacts on our ability as parents to stay within our window of tolerance. It is at these times when we feel overwhelmed by our children's behaviour that our window of tolerance reduces. Parents may feel that their 'buttons are being pushed', they may get mad and feel that they can't seem to stop. In these situations, when the parent–child relationship becomes disconnected it is important to question what is being triggered in ourselves and identify how we are feeling.

At times, particularly when our own unresolved issues are being triggered by a child's behaviour, our responses can become inflexible. This response inflexibility is often an indication that one's window of tolerance is collapsing. When a window of tolerance collapses we feel overwhelmed with feelings of fear, sadness and anger. When this happens we are less able to attune to our children. These intense and often overwhelming emotional responses occur as the connections to the cortex, the rational area of the brain, become blocked, leading to *reactive* as opposed to *thoughtful* responses. When we are no longer mindful in our parenting, nurturing and connecting communication is unlikely and instead relationship ruptures are likely to occur. At these times we are operating from an emotional mind.

When we operate outside of our window of tolerance we may find ourselves frequently trapped into an unsatisfying and repetitive cycle of poor communication with our children. This *escalation trap* can be particularly frightening and confusing for the preschool-age child. Escalation traps are characterised by loud, rigid, critical, shaming and angry exchanges. For example, a parent may state, 'you need to… ' the child responds, 'no', and the parent then uses a loud voice, 'do it now or else….' The child cries and then screams 'I hate you' and the parent may shout in an angry tone 'I hate you too' and smack the child.

Having unresolved issues of your own makes you more vulnerable to having a small window of tolerance under stressful situations. By reflecting on your own experiences you can prevent yourself from returning time and time again to this escalation trap. By increasing our understanding of ourselves and our past experiences we can improve our resilience and reduce the likelihood of continued relationship rupture. In other words, we can increase our own window of tolerance.

A large window of tolerance allows us to activate rationale and reflective thought processes. Such thought processes are sometimes referred to as a *wise mind*. When we use a wise mind we are operating within our window of tolerance, which allows us to reflect on possibilities and to respond considerately, while applying consequences to our children's behaviour. A spacious window of tolerance gives us the tools to be flexible in our choices and ultimately to be the type of parent we want to be. It doesn't mean that we will have conflict free relationships with our preschool-age children however it does allow us to choose how we respond to their inconsiderate behaviour. By being planned and intentional in our thoughtful communication and actions we are able to foster a healthy loving supportive relationship with our preschool-age child.

Cultivating emotional intelligence

Through compassionate and assertive parenting we can facilitate the successful development of our child's window of tolerance and the development of their emotional intelligence and whole brain. Children with a large window of tolerance are able to regulate and control their impulses, delay gratification, motivate themselves, read others' social cues and cope with life's ups and downs.

Children's window of tolerance develops throughout childhood and is very small in children in the early years. The development of a spacious and flexible window of tolerance occurs when parents are able to acknowledge and reflect their children's feelings. Parents who fail to teach their children emotional intelligence tend to have parenting practices which are:

- dismissive (they ignore or trivialise emotions),
- disapproving (they are critical or punishing), or
- laissez-faire (they empathise but fail to offer guidance or set limits).

Parents who are effective emotion coaches are able to:

- acknowledge and label a child's feeling (anger/sadness).
- help them name it,
- allow the child to experience the feelings,
- stay close while the child feels the feeling (rages/cries), and
- set limits.

When children have a consistent experience of having their feelings validated and acknowledged they are emotionally healthier and more resilient. As a parent it is okay to express emotions but the key is to express them in ways that are not destructive to your relationship with your child. By expressing these feelings you show your child that strong feelings can be expressed and managed and that your child's behaviour matters to you. *Affirming messages* (positive comments) are validating and not only support the parent–child relationship but also help children achieve the developmental tasks of their current life stage.

Affirming messages during the early years

Affirming message are positive, supporting verbal statements and thoughts. Children are affirmed when:
- their questions are answered,
- their imagination is encouraged,
- their appropriate behaviour is acknowledged, and
- their inconsiderate behaviour is managed effectively.

Affirming messages are essential health-giving statements that children need throughout life (Illsley Clark, 1994). When affirming messages are authentic they are sincere and believable to children.

Affirming messages need to match the child's age and stage and should fit with their developmental tasks. Infants are in a developmental period of learning to trust and find ways to have their needs met. Toddlers (from six to eighteen months) are learning to trust their senses and explore their environment. During this time they are developing their intelligence, sense of self, identity and the ability to be independent. As children move towards two years of age, they enter the thinking stage of development. They become more autonomous and not only learn to think for themselves but also to establish cause-and-effect thinking (one action results in another). Children at this age may often explore anger and resistance. By the age of three to five years they are exploring their identity and experimenting with being powerful. During this preschool-age period children learn socially appropriate ways of behaving and actively try out different ways of relating.

Figure 3.1 on pages 32–35 lists appropriate affirming messages along with both helpful and unhelpful behaviour for each stage of a young child's develeopment (adapted from Illsley, Clark & Dawson, 1998).

As parents, it is our job to cultivate confidence, perseverance, resilience, accountability, social adaptability, and a spacious and flexible window of tolerance in our children. These things will help them move towards independence and responsibility. When children fully believe they are unconditionally loved and that their parents will consistently set clear, loving, firm and predictable limits, their brains can grow. They can go about their important developmental tasks and learn to be independent thinkers, with strong self-esteem and self-efficacy.

Building your bag of tricks

Flexible, mindful responding is about having a bag of tricks to assist you in your parenting. The bag of tricks approach to parenting is aimed at parents being able to maintain their emotional equilibrium while remaining flexible in their approach. Parents effectively become emotion coaches for their children. When we are flexible in our parenting we are better able to make decisions about how to choose to manage our children's behaviour. Flexible parents generally have a large window of tolerance and are able to foster their child's emotional intelligence and self-esteem.

You need to be aware of the following when building your bag of tricks:

- The path to becoming the best parent you can be begins with self-examination.

Stage of development	Job of the child	Typical behaviours of the child	Affirmations for being	Helpful parent behaviours	Unhelpful parent behaviours
Birth to 6 months (Being)	To call for care To cry to get needs met To accept touch To accept nurturance To bond emotionally—to learn to trust caring adults and self To be	Cries to make needs known Cuddles Makes lots of sounds Looks at and responds to faces Imitates	'I'm glad you are in my life' 'You belong here' 'What you need is important to me' 'I'm glad you are you' 'You can grow at your own pace' 'You can feel all of your feelings' 'I love you and I care for you willingly'	Affirm the infant for doing developmental tasks Provide loving, consistent care Respond to the baby's needs Think for the infant Hold and look at the baby while feeding Nurture by touching, looking, talking and singing Get help when unsure of how to provide care Be reliable and trustworthy Get others to nurture you	Ignoring the baby's signals Not touching or holding enough Rigid, angry and agitated responses Feeding before the baby signals Punishment Lack of a healthy physical environment Lack of protection Criticising the infant Discounting
6 to 18 months (Doing)	To explore and experience the environment To develop sensory awareness by using all senses To signal needs; to trust others and self To continue forming secure attachments with parents To get help in times of stress To start to learn that there	Tests all senses by exploring the environment Is curious Is easily distracted Wants to explore on own but be able to retrieve caregiver at will Starts playing 'peek-a-boo' etc Starts using words during middle or latter part of this	'I will support and protect you and you can explore and experiment' 'You can use all of your senses when you explore' 'You can do things as many times as you need to' 'You can know what you know' 'You can be interested in	Affirm child for doing developmental tasks Continue to offer love, safety, and protection Provide a safe environment Protect child from harm Continue to provide food, nurturing non-sexual touch and encouragement	Failure to provide protection Restriction of mobility Criticism or shame in response to exploring or doing Discipline or punishment Expecting child not to touch 'precious' objects Expecting toilet training

Figure 3.1(a) Development and affirming messages

Chapter 3 Raising Emotionally Intelligent Children

age	tasks	stage	affirming messages	Discounting
	are options and not all problems are easily solved To develop initiative To continue tasks from the Being stage		everything' 'I like to watch you grow and learn' 'I love you when you are active or quiet'	Say two 'yeses' for every 'no' Provide a variety of things for the child to experience Refrain from interrupting child when possible Refrain from interpreting the child's behaviour—'You like looking at yourself in the mirror' Instead, report the child's behaviour—'Sarah is looking in the mirror' Respond when child initiates play Take care of own needs	
18 months to 3 years (Thinking)	To establish ability to think for self To test reality, to push against boundaries and other people To learn to think and solve problems with cause and effect thinking To start to follow simple commands To express anger and other feelings To separate from parents	Begins cause and effect thinking Starts parallel play Starts to be orderly, even compulsive Sometimes follows simple commands, sometimes resists Tests behaviours: 'No, I won't, and you can't make me' Some try out the use of tantrums	'I'm glad you are starting to think for yourself' 'It's okay for you to be angry, but I won't let you hurt yourself or others' 'You can say 'no' and push and test limits as much as you need to' 'You can learn to think for yourself and I will think for myself' 'You can think and feel at the same time'	Affirm child for doing developmental tasks Continue to offer cuddling, love, safety and protection Celebrate the child's new thinking ability Encourage cause and effect thinking Provide reasons, how to's, and other information Accept positive and negative expression of feelings Teach options for expressing	Using too many don'ts and not enough do's Getting caught in power struggles Trying to appear to be a good parent by having a compliant child Referring to the child as a 'terrible two' Not setting limits or expectations Setting too high expectations Expecting the child to play

Figure 3.1(b) Development and affirming messages

Age	Development		Affirming messages	Helpful behaviours	Unhelpful behaviours
				without losing their love To start to give up beliefs about being the centre of the universe To continue tasks from earlier stages	'You can know what you need and ask for help' 'You can become separate from me and I will still love you'	feelings instead of hurting or tantruming Set reasonable limits and adhere to them Remain constant in face of child's outbursts and inconsiderate behaviour; neither give in nor overpower Provide time and space for child to organise thinking Give simple, clear directions that can be followed; encourage and praise achievement Expect them to think about their own feelings and start to think about those of others Think of and refer to the child as a 'Terrific Two' Take care of own needs	'with' other children before learning to play 'near' others (parallel play) Reluctance to manage inconsiderate behaviour Shaming the child Discounting
3 to 6 years (Identity and Power)	To assert an identity separate from others To acquire information about the world, themselves and their body To learn that behaviors have consequences To discover their effect on	Engages in fantasy play, possibly with imaginary companions Gathers information: how, why, when, how long, etc Trys different identity roles by roleplaying Starts learning about power relationships by watching and	'You can explore who you are and find out who other people are' 'You can be powerful and ask for help at the same time' 'You can try out different roles and ways of being powerful' 'You can learn the results of	Affirm children for doing developmental tasks Continus to offer love, safety and protection Provide support as the child explores the world of things, people, ideas and feelings Encourage the child to enjoy being a boy, or a girl; teach	Teasing Inconsistency Not expecting child to think for self Unwillingness to answer questions Ridicules child for role-playing or fantasies

Figure 3.1(c) Development and affirming messages

others	setting up power struggles	your behaviour'	that both sexes are okay	Responds to child's fantasies as if real
To learn to exert power to affect relationships	Practices behaviours for sex role identification	'All of your feelings are okay with me'	Expect the child to express feelings and to connect feelings and thinking	Use of fantasy to frighten or confuse
To practise considerate and socially appropriate behaviour	Starts cooperative play	'You can learn what is pretend and what is real'	Provide information about the child's environment and correct misinformation	Discounting
To separate fantasy from reality	Practices considerate and socially appropriate behaviour	'Your enthusiasm is valued and respected'	Answer questions	
To learn what they have power over and what they do not have power over	Begins demonstrating interest in games and roles	'You are fun to be with'	Provide appropriate consequences for actions	
To continue learning earlier developmental tasks		'I love who you are'	Use language that is clear	
			Encourage fantasy as well as the separation of fantasy and reality	
			Acknowledge appropriate and considerate behaviour	
			Respond accurately to curiosity about the human body, boys and girls	
			Maintain contact with supportive people who help nurture you as a parent	

Figure 3.1(d) Development and affirming messages

- Parents' own childhood experiences can impact on their reactions to their children.
- It is important that parents accept negative emotions in their children as part of life and use these as an opportunity to teach important life skills.
- Warm and positive parenting alone does not teach emotional intelligence — parents need to deal with children's negative emotions while staying regulated and within their own window of tolerance.
- Children learn more from what you do and how you look, than what you say.
- A window of tolerance is ultimately the ability to think and feel at the same time — for children this is the ability to react and not overreact to daily events.
- Parents who are reflective in their parenting are more likely to have a positive and happy relationship with their children.
- A strong attachment relationship between children and their parents will support the development of a spacious window of tolerance and form the scaffolding on which parent management techniques can be built.

BAG OF TRICKS

1. **Be aware of children's emotions.**
   Use opportunities for intimacy and teaching. Listen with empathy and validate your child's feelings. Help them find the words to label their emotions. Set limits while exploring strategies to solve the problem.

2. **Don't discount children's feelings.**
   Just because they are smaller, less rational, less experienced and less powerful than adults doesn't mean their feelings are less real or intense.

3. **Communicate effectively.**
   Communication that acknowledges a child's feelings lays the foundation for lifelong relationships.

4. **Be aware of your level of emotional arousal and needs.**
   Stay engaged if you think you can be rational, or if you're too mad, take a break and discuss issues later. It is also important to take a break if you think you'll say something destructive, hit or insult your child.

5. **Be aware.**
   Understand your own reactions to the strong feelings your children's behaviour evokes in you.

6. **Ask for support and help.**
   If you need support and to assist you with responding to your children in a positive, nurturing and mindful way then seek it out.

7. **Practise mindfulness.**
   Stop, breathe, respond.

Chapter 4

Responding to Your Child's Developmental Needs

For children in the early years the parent–child relationship is central to their sense of safety and security. Confidence and security is built when parents are able to respond to their child's needs for play and exploration while at the same time helping them to regulate their negative emotional states and move towards positive outcomes. It is essential that the child in the early years is developmentally able to cope with expectations and that parents are aware that their limit setting will be tested many times.

Unfortunately, in some situations the developmental tasks of children in the early years are misunderstood and interpreted as 'bad' behaviour. When this occurs children are reprimanded for normal and developmentally appropriate actions. For example parents can express frustration at the constant movement and climbing of a toddler in the Doing Phase of development (6–18 months of age) or the emotionality of a child in the Thinking Phase (18 months to three years of age) who is learning to express and manage strong feelings. For many parents as their children develop into the preschool years (3 to 6 years of age) their identity development and need to figure out power relationships becomes a central feature of their development and escalation traps can occur.

Negativism is a normal part of children's developing self-awareness and is apparent in children from 12 to 18 months usually easing as the child nears three years of age. During this developmental phase toddlers are easily frustrated and are hard to regulate. The testing nature of toddlers' behaviour and their determination to try things on their own, can be dysregulating for parents and can actually trigger their own emotions. Aggressiveness, although worrying to parents, is a normal developmental occurrence and passes as the development expands into another way of behaving.

Emotions can be regulated by the use of the word 'we' and by the imposition of consistent and predictable routines. If routines are kept fun and 'we' is not overly used, toddlers who are focused on 'me' will be able to be assisted to regulate during moments of emotional turmoil. The use of a calm matter-of-fact voice assists in reregulating toddler's emotional states and is helpful in not reinforcing difficult behaviour.

Children during this developmental phase need to be transitioned to another activity or task otherwise they will continue to fight to have their way. Parents who are sensitive and matter-of-fact are in a better position to have flexible approaches to helping their child to cooperate without becoming emotionally dysregulated themselves. They are able to stay within their own window of tolerance. Situations that may occur include: a toddler not wanting to share their toys, not wanting to go to bed or not wanting to stop their play to eat dinner.

Toddlers view the world through their experience of it and they very much live in the present, finding it difficult to wait for anything. Their feeling states change rapidly and they do not typically manage transitions with ease. Announcing transitions (for example, getting in the car, going to the shops, coming home from the park) before they actually happen is an effective strategy and helps the toddler to see the next step, allowing them to move on from what they are doing at that moment in time. Statements that effectively announce the next interesting step are helpful in moving the toddler from one activity or exercise to another: 'It's time to go now. When we get home, we can blow bubbles in the garden.'

Children in the early years often try to do things themselves. By encouraging their exploration, problem-solving, and helping when things don't go as expected, you can continue to support their secure relationship with you. The use of *choice statements* in particular both guides your child and supports their independence, for example, 'Do you want to wear your blue socks or your new purple ones?' Such choice statements give children a sense of power. This is important to preschool children who are increasingly aware that they are their own person.

It is normal for preschool-aged children to try to test their parents and their own capabilities. They like to be in charge and to make their own decisions. Themes of power and control are present in much of their play and imaginary games. Pretend play is a child's way of trying out new roles and making sense of what is real and what is imaginary. Creativity should be encouraged and this is a time where children learn about the many options life has to offer through their play.

Toddlers and preschool-aged children are egocentric and find sharing hard. Many do not start sharing easily until well into their primary schooling. Sharing is a very mature concept but one children need to learn how to handle. Talking about sharing is one way to help children hear and learn this important skill. Thus, the toddler who has just snatched their toy from a baby sibling, who is now upset, can be approached with statements about their emotions and desires while also offering a solution. For example:

> *I know you wanted your toy back, but Sam was playing with it when you grabbed it from him. You can let him play with it for a few minutes while you play with something else, or you can give him another toy to play with.*

Statements like this teach the child how to solve problems, and with time can lead to avoidance of future conflict. Through talking and listening the child learns to solve such problems for themselves.

Sharing is a learned behaviour and understanding comes with time. As children near their fifth year they may start to identify one special friend and perhaps start to share. At this time is can be useful if there is an adult close by to help them negotiate tricky moments.

As preschool-aged children move into their fourth year it becomes more evident that they like to do things their way. They also have a much longer concentration span than when they were three years old. They thrive on acknowledgement and seek to please their parents. When they know that they have done so, they feel proud and happy. Nevertheless, they also like to repeatedly test the limits of parental expectations and to ask 'why?'. They have a sense of outrage and can be very dramatic and display big emotions. They like to have things their own way and they will often say when rules are broken.

As children get ready to start primary school they like to show off what they can do and may embellish stories. Such embellishment may sound like lies to us, particularly as their imagination gets the better of them. They may also lie to try to cover up mistakes made or to test expectations and boundaries. Parents can avoid escalation traps by asking the child if it is a 'true' or 'pretend story'. If handled with gentleness and not made to be the focus of attention, embellishment or lying is likely to significantly decrease. Useful statements at this time include: 'You make up amazing stories but right now I need you to answer me'.

Commonly misunderstood behaviours

Parenting children in the early years is a demanding and busy time. For many parents developmentally normal behaviour in their children can be misunderstood as 'naughty'. When this happens toddler and preschool-age children can be punished for simply going about their developmental tasks. It is thus essential that parents are aware of developmental tasks during these early years and so react accordingly. Appropriate limit setting allows children to be protected while also being independent.

Six to eighteen months old

- The toddler is learning to explore and trust their environment. They are not deliberately making mess or breaking things on purpose. During this developmental phase the child's environment needs to be child friendly so that parents do not need to constantly limit exploratory play.
- Toddlers are active and curious. Such constant activity and curiosity can be dysregulating (that is, upsetting, frustrating, even stressful) for parents, particularly when they themselves are tired or exhausted.
- The toddler begins to need time and space away from others to develop and test their separateness and individuality. During this developmental phase it is important not to emotionally reject the child or perceive their developing autonomy as rejection of you.

- Aggressive behaviour is common in children from nine months to three years of age. This occurs because children in this developmental phase live in the moment, are experimenting, curious, egocentric and have no understanding of cause and effect. Adequate supervision of toddlers and preschool-aged children helps to ensure there is less likelihood of aggressive behaviour. Effective parenting requires parents to actively participate and redirect activities where necessary and to reinforce and acknowledge non-aggressive behaviour. It is counterproductive to focus on how upsetting the behaviour is for others as the child is more interested in parental approval than how others feel.
- Taking out anger and frustration on toys is a way in which children under two years of age act out their feelings and learn to manage their strong emotions. By ignoring the aggression and focusing on the positive, pro-social behaviour is reinforced: 'Lucky teddy got a kiss. You are such a kind girl.'
- As the toddler develops into the preschool years it is crucial for parents to remember that they are an individual and not an extension of the parent. Follow the child's lead in determining their interests and help them to build on their skills.
- Toddler's memory is developing. Thus, memory of cause and effect is limited.

Eighteen months old to two years old

- Saying 'no' is how a child learns to become separate from their parent. This necessary developmental task of resisting a parent can be misunderstood as defiance. If it is managed with aggression or anger by the parent the child is left feeling powerless and fearful. Alternatively if it is not

managed assertively and decisively the child learns that throwing a tantrum is a way to get what they want.
- Despite developing autonomy toddlers still require structure and boundaries in order to develop well. Parents who have clear and predictable expectations and limits, and communicate these effectively, allow their child to meet their developmental trajectory. They also have a bag of tricks to use which makes it less likely that they themselves will be dysregulated by their child's behaviour.
- It is important that toddlers' strong emotions are managed calmly. If they are managed in an angry fashion this will trigger the downstairs brain (limbic system) and cause further fighting and distress. The goal is to help them to feel safe, for example, not just to stop them crying. Useful statements include: 'I know it's not working, Mum is here...'
- Toddlers learn fast. However, their eagerness to do things can exceed their ability. When this occurs they may become frustrated. Many frustrations have an obvious cause, such as throwing a teddy bear because its clothes won't go on or kicking a safety gate that is blocking their way up stairs. Meeting children's efforts half way can help to overcome the frustration without disempowering them. Children predominantly learn through what they see others doing. Therefore it is crucial that parents and other adults model calm problem solving.
- Toddlers and preschool-aged children do not deliberately 'wind up' their parents. Children's behaviour always has a reason behind it. Although it may not always be immediately clear, try to understand the reason behind any behaviour before judging it as problematic. By being aware of a child's behavioural traits and the signals that

they use to express their needs, wants and moods, parents are more able to understand what is behind the behavioural response.
- Difficulty with toilet training is common in children as they move into the preschool years. They need to be in charge of their body. When children initiate toilet training themselves they can have more success at mastering this competency and developing appropriate toilet habits. Such habits are not easy to acquire under duress or during conflict.

Three to five years old

- The memory of children in their preschool years is more reliable than during their earlier development.
- Preschool-age children need to be taught how to play appropriately with their younger siblings. Supportive assistance in helping children to play greatly facilitates this. Useful statements include: 'Three-year-olds are good at building tall towers, your sister is good at knocking them down. Toddlers like to put blocks in a container. Let's find something you can do with her.' In supporting appropriate play, you set the scene for paying attention to desirable behaviour.
- Children in the early years are learning the difference between fantasy and reality. This ability to fully distinguish between the two is not completely developed until they are about seven years of age. It is normal for children to be confused about what is real and what is make-believe. They may also have a tendency to experiment with what is true and what is not. Parents and caring adults can explain to children what a lie is and that there is a family expectation that everyone tells the truth. However, it is crucial that if a

parent suspects that their child is embellishing or lying that they do not overreact. By simply asking the child if it is a 'true story' or a 'pretend story', escalation and shaming can be avoided. In addition, knowing that this is part of normal development and that it will change over time allows for less attention to be given to such stories.
- Preschool-aged children have the developmental task of testing their power and being powerful. When parents remain in charge they are able to avoid power struggles with their child. The use of humour, distraction, planned ignoring, affirming messages and effective instructions all allow the child to go about their developmental tasks without parental misinterpretation. If you assertively manage the use of swear words and comments like, 'I don't like you' the behaviour will be quickly extinguished. Try saying things like, 'If you'd like to use rude words, please go into the bathroom and close the door, I do not want to hear them.' A statement such as 'No one in our family is stupid' gives a clear message of what is expected.
- Children this age may still have issues with their toileting. Parents who recognise that children have a right to be in charge of their own bodies support the development of independent toileting.
- As rational thinking develops in the preschool-age child it is important not to expect behaviour that is above the child's developmental capacity.

Encouraging desirable behaviour

Children in the early years exhibit challenging behaviour. Parents typically talk about how their children always want their own way, are not able to tolerate the word 'no', are naughty, have tantrums, don't seem to get on with other children, can't seem to share, don't follow simple instructions, do the opposite of what they are asked and generally won't cooperate. Such challenging behaviour occurs because the emotional centres of the brain are more developed than the thinking parts of the brain at a time when children are learning about the rules of behaviour.

During the early years parents can fall into the trap of managing children's challenging behaviour in punitive ways. Acknowledging desirable behaviour is as effective, if not more so, than punishing bad behaviour. It helps children learn how to behave in appropriate ways. Essentially children do not naturally know how to behave and considerate behaviour needs to be taught. When children are rewarded for appropriate behaviour they learn socially appropriate ways of behaving. The more a child's appropriate behaviour is acknowledged, the less they will be attracted to doing things that are not acknowledged. By focusing on positive one-on-one time the parent–child relationship is strengthened and supports the child in making pro-social choices.

Child-centred time

Children need one-on-one time with their parents. Child-centred time does not have to be for long periods, but it must be spent between just you and your child preferably doing something they enjoy. Interruptions should be avoided, as the aim of this process is for your child to have your complete and undivided attention. Having this one-on-one time regularly will limit your child's need to gain attention by engaging in inconsiderate behaviour.

Child-centred time can be both structured and unstructured. Parents can spend a lot of time and effort thinking of special activities or events they can do with their child, when often the simple things can be most effective. Special time can be just sitting with your child and reading with them or drawing pictures together, playing with playdough or doing puzzles. Remember it's the time spent together that is the focus, not the activity.

Structured child-centred time involves setting aside five to ten minutes of intensive time to play with your child, where they lead the activity by choosing *what* they would like to play with and how they'd like to play. Your role is to join in, encourage and acknowledge appropriate and considerate behaviour. It is important to avoid giving instructions ('It's best if you do it like this'), asking questions ('Why have you done this?' 'What are you doing?' 'Are you having fun?') or criticising ('I can't believe you can't…').

There are many benefits to giving a child attention when you are able. Often it means they will be less likely to demand attention when you are not able to give it. Child-centred time strengthens the relationship between a child and parent, making children feel secure and creating the foundation for dealing with conflict and inconsiderate behaviour. The one-on-one attention also tends to improve children's language development, play skills and concentration span. Many parents find that through child-centred time their children gain more ideas about how to play and are then able to spend more time entertaining themselves. Ultimately this time improves children's self-esteem and self-worth.

Building your bag of tricks

Child-centred time takes practice. Most parents find the bag-of-tricks strategies outlined below difficult to apply at first — engaging in child-centred playtime is not easy. As adults, it is hard not to ask questions and easy to miss opportunities to acknowledge and encourage. Don't be discouraged. As with any new skill, it takes time and practice.

BAG OF TRICKS

1. **Step one.**
   Decide on a time each day that will be your 'special' time with your child. Aim to set aside around five to ten minutes. This time should not be dependent on good behaviour. Remember not all child-centred time needs to be planned. Look for opportunities to spend time with your child throughout the day: reading in the morning before day care, sitting and having a drink and a snack together after preschool and talking about their day.

2. **Step two.**
   'Special' time is one-on-one time. If you have other children in the family, it is important to find someone else (such as your partner) to look after them. Alternatively you can choose a time when they are unlikely to disturb the activity.

3. **Step three.**
   Choose a time when you are able to relax and give your full attention to your child.

4. **Step four.**
   If you have a set time, you can say to your child, 'It's our special time to be together, what would you like to do?' Aim to have only a few toys or activities out at a time. Books, drawing materials, playdough and creative toys are particularly suited to child-centred time. If you do not have a special playtime, then approach your child while they are playing alone and ask if you can join in.

5. **Step five.**
   Try to avoid toys that encourage rough or aggressive play (such as bats and balls); activities that could get out of hand (such as paints); and games that have pre-set rules. The aim is to set up a play situation that makes it easy for your child to behave calmly and considerately.

6. **Step six.**
   After watching your child's play for a couple of minutes, describe what they are doing, for example:

   'You are building a tower.'

   'You're drawing in blue crayon.'

Chapter 4 Responding to Your Child's Developmental Needs

'You're making lots of balls with the playdough.'

This shows the child that you are interested and will help to hold their attention.

7. **Step seven.**
Look for opportunities to reflect your child's language, for example:

Child: 'I'm drawing a rainbow.'

Parent: 'Yes, you're using the red.'

Child: 'I like to play with the playdough.'

Parent: 'It's a fun to play with.'

This shows your child that you are really listening and that you understand and accept what they are doing.

8. **Step eight.**
After a while, join in by copying appropriate play, for example:

Child: 'I'm going to make spaghetti.'

Parent: 'I'm going to make a pizza.'

Child: 'I'm drawing a flower.'

Parent: 'I'm going to draw a flower in my picture too.'

This shows your child that you are involved and teaches them to play with others.

9. **Step nine.**
Find opportunities to acknowledge your child, for example:

'That's a colourful picture.'

'You're playing so quietly.'

'Thank you for sharing the pencils with me.'

'I really enjoy it when we play together.'

This adds to the warmth of the relationship and will help to increase your child's self-esteem.

10. **Step ten.**
Avoid commands and questions during child-centred time. These prevent your child from leading the play and can make the playtime feel too parent driven. Ignore

inappropriate behaviour (for example, talking back) unless it is dangerous or destructive. Do this by looking away for a moment. If your child engages in dangerous or destructive behaviour (for example, hitting), tell them that the playtime is over and leave the room. Tell them that you will play later when they are able to participate appropriately. This avoids increasing inappropriate or inconsiderate behaviour (by withdrawing attention) and will help your child to see the difference in your response to considerate and inconsiderate behaviour.

Chapter 5

Acknowledging Desirable Behaviour and Reflecting Feelings

Children's dependency on affection and approval often translates into an intense need for attention from their parents and significant others. Children strive for attention whether it is positive or negative. When attention is rare, they may see any attention as better than none at all. The attention-gaining techniques we see children display are subconscious, outside their awareness, and can become a habit very quickly.

Parents also have behaviour patterns that they are unaware of. As parents our response to children's behaviour trains them to respond to situations in different ways. For example, if a child is usually gentle with their baby sibling and you fail to acknowledge this and only respond negatively when they are rough, then you are unintentionally training your child that it is negative behaviour that will gain your attention. Forgetting to notice the positives and focusing heavily on the negatives is easy to do and leads to conflict in the parent–child relationship. Breaking this negative cycle by acknowledging desirable behaviour is a powerful technique to change negative behaviour patterns and increase the behaviours you want to see more of.

Effective acknowledgement

When children feel good about what they do, they will seek to do it more regularly. With time this behaviour becomes established and automatic. Paying attention to behaviours increases the likelihood that you will see them more often. As such, acknowledgement is one of the most powerful ways to influence your child's behaviour. It is also an important way to help a child grow in confidence and self-esteem.

Children need frequent acknowledgement so that they can learn what considerate behaviour is. This is particularly important during the early years because children of that age are at a developmental phase where they are learning what is acceptable and what is not. Acknowledgement reinforces pro-social and considerate behaviour, encourages learning and also sets a standard for what is achievable.

Acknowledgement can be either general or descriptive. General acknowledgement is vague (for example, 'that's great', 'good boy', 'well done') and doesn't convey to the child what they have done or how it has impacted upon anyone else. Descriptive or labelled acknowledgement is clear and specific. It tells your child exactly what it is that they have done:

'Thank you for coming to the table when you were asked.'

'Well done for keeping your hands and feet to yourself.'

'Thank you for calming down and using your words.'

These statements help children to change their behaviour because they indicate exactly which behaviours are appropriate.

To effectively acknowledge your child, you need to catch them behaving considerately — even if it is only for a small moment in a long period of undesirable behaviour.

Ways to acknowledge

Acknowledge your child for doing something positive with simple words and your body language; a smile and/or words, for example: 'That was a really nice thing you just did, sharing with your sister.'

Be wary of the temptation to reward your child for considerate behaviour with material things. By simply acknowledging their behaviour, you are making them feel noticed and validated. Children are quick to notice acknowledgement that is insincere or over the top and it can at times have an unintentional negative effect.

The application of acknowledgement allows children to know what the positive behaviour was, and the attention from doing it will make them want to repeat the behaviour. Sometimes acknowledgement can feel clichéd or unnatural. Finding your own phrases or terms that you feel comfortable with will ensure that your acknowledgement remains sincere.

The more often you acknowledge the positive actions of your child, the more likely they are to understand what it is you expect of them. As a result, you are more likely to see more considerate behaviour and fewer behavioural errors. As parents, we need to understand that everything we say can be internalised by our children. This is especially important when we use labels to convey expectations. If we label our child as naughty enough times, they will begin to believe it and will act accordingly. Labelling behaviour can also be a positive tool. If we consistently tell our child that they are gentle or fun to be with, they will continue to practise traits identified with this. The following ideas may help you to create your own statements to use with your children.

Labelled acknowledgement ideas
- 'Thank you for using your big voice.'
- 'You're fun to be with.'
- 'I like the way that you were able to sit with the baby and play nicely with her.'
- 'You're doing a great job of speaking with an inside voice.'

- 'I like the way you came to the table straight away.'
- 'It's a pleasure to cuddle with you when you use your gentle touch.'
- 'You did a great job of getting your shoes just now.'
- 'Thank you for sitting at the table.'
- 'You're doing a great job of paying attention.'
- 'Thank you for sharing.'
- 'You're being a kind sister.'
- 'You are doing a great job of taking turns.'
- 'Thank you for quietly listening.'
- 'You are drawing very carefully.'
- 'Thank you for waiting for your turn.'
- 'I liked the way you helped me in the garden today.'
- 'You did a great job helping me to…'
- 'You did well to stay in bed.'

It can be powerfully reinforcing for preschool-aged children to overhear you telling another person about their behaviour ('I was so proud watching Sam being such a kind big brother today'), or for another person to comment to them at a later time about what they have heard said about their considerate behaviour ('Your mum told me that you did great listening today, I'm so proud of you'). You can use family members such as partners, grandparents or other adult friends to practise this method of acknowledging considerate behaviour.

Proximity

The verbal information that we share (the words that we use) is only a small component of how we communicate. Non-verbal messages such as eye contact, tone of voice, body posture, facial expression and the timing and intensity of response, all show a lot about what we are feeling and thinking.

Differences between non-verbal (body language) and verbal communication are confusing to infants and children in the early years. In fact, because of the way the brain develops babies, toddlers and preschool-aged children require primarily non-verbal (right brain) communication. This need for non-verbal communication means moving physically closer to a young child when you are talking to them and works better than simply explaining your point in words.

The use of proximity is effective in both 'up-regulating' and 'down-regulating' a child's feeling state. Emotion regulation, in turn, is highly associated with secure attachment. Through the effective use of proximity and attunement (discussed in chapter 2) parents can co-regulate their child's emotions until they are developmentally ready and able to self-regulate.

Attachment rich and attachment neutral engagement

Getting attention can be one of the main reasons that children misbehave. One effective way to reinforce desirable behaviour that utilises the child's desire for attention is to use attention itself. The fundamental principal behind parental attention is that behaviours that are recognised and paid attention to will be seen more often. Unfortunately parents more commonly pay attention to behaviours that are annoying or wrong, ultimately reinforcing the behaviours that are unwanted.

Parental reactions of displeasure often increase the likelihood of further negative behaviour. Aversive discipline interchanges, when frequent, are attachment rich and contain basic attachment drives in the child, which often results in them continuing to escalate. When this *attachment rich reinforcement* continues for negative behaviours, positive interchanges become increasingly infrequent and attachment neutral, further escalating the situation. Parents can thus fall into a trap in which they provide very little attention to desirable behaviour and lots of engagement for inconsiderate behaviour. When this is the typical dynamic in a family a *reinforcement trap* develops — parents engage with misbehaviour, therefore the child gets more attention for negative behaviour than for positive behaviour and the negative behaviour increases.

Attachment rich engagement not only occurs when there is a negative reinforcement trap but also when parents are animated and loud. These are usually in times of excitement but can also be at times of stress such as when children are behaving badly. Such loud exchanges are negatively reinforcing because they activate basic attachment drives in the child. Just as our passion and excitement are infectious and reinforcing, our anger can be negatively reinforcing, ultimately increasing the likelihood of seeing more of the inappropriate or unproductive behaviour.

Children in the early years have trouble differentiating between positive and negative attention. As such it is very easy to negatively reinforce undesirable behaviour. Negative reinforcement includes:

- shouting
- smacking
- inconsistent management of undesirable behaviour such as tantrums, screaming, whinging, nagging, night sleep issues and rough play with younger siblings.

Additionally, nagging, shaming, humiliating, threatening punishment with no intention of follow-through and being overly protective and accommodating of negative behaviour are all reinforcing. The key here is to make the consequences for inconsiderate behaviour dull, boring and impersonal and shift the focus to times of appropriate behaviour.

Be consistent

Remember, behaviours that receive attention increase. Pick three or four target desired behaviours and get ready to 'catch' your child doing them so you can acknowledge and positively reinforce them.

Examples of commonly desired behaviours include:

- good listening
- gentle touch
- calm voice
- using a big girl/boy voice
- holding hands when out
- sitting in the car seat
- staying in bed
- following instructions
- keeping hands and feet to self.

Reflecting feelings

It is critical that we nurture the development of emotional understanding and compassion for our children. Having conversations with our children about their thoughts, feelings and memory provides them with interpersonal experiences that are necessary for building social skills and self-understanding. Children who have learnt how to openly express their feelings are better equipped to manage conflict. A child's emotional state can be regulated through the use of the relationship between parent and child. When adults are able to engage children in this way, children feel heard.

Emotional connections with others are formed through the sharing of emotions. By attuning to the emotional experience of your child you allow them to feel heard. Children show how they are feeling through the behaviour that they exhibit. Often parents react to behaviour and do not recognise that such behaviour is an expression of a child's emotional needs. Recognising that there are hidden feelings and needs allows parents to respond appropriately to their child's emotionality. Understanding the situation from the child's perspective and the meaning behind their behaviour helps parents to be able to manage their child's behaviour in a mindful and calm manner. With time children can learn to regulate their behaviour because they have experienced being soothed and regulated by a caring and calm adult.

Labelling feelings is the first step in managing challenging behaviour and gives the child the message that their ideas, needs and emotions are valued. When a child's experience is validated and an attuned adult has reflected their feelings to them, the child is able to integrate their experience by essentially reflecting on their internal and external world. Such integrating reflection allows parents to support their children's development in a responsive and mutually collaborative way thereby helping the child to make sense of the communication.

The emotions of children in the early years are immediate and they have a tendency to oscillate between the intense feelings of love and hate. By being able to emotionally reflect back to a preschool-age child, parents are able to remain emotionally regulated themselves. In staying emotionally regulated themselves, parents are able to remain in charge of the situation and allow the child to feel safe in their feeling of strong emotions.

Children in the early years are experimenting with anger and learning how parents respond to this emotion. Reflecting feelings allows the child to know that you see their anger, that you are not afraid of it, and that you love them even when they are angry. Through acknowledging and reflecting strong feelings children learn effective ways to manage and stay regulated. It is not uncommon for children to say 'I hate you' when they do not get what they want. Statements that reflect back to the child include:

- 'Yes, I get you hate me right now.'
- 'Kids get mad at mums sometimes, but you are not to run away.'
- 'We are your family and we must learn to get along.'
- 'I can see that you are upset. It is okay to be mad.'

The ability to perceive the internal experience of another person allows us to be compassionate. The development of empathy or the ability to understand the internal world of another is promoted when children have had experience of having their feelings validated. Parents who reflect their child's feelings help them to make sense of the internal processes that are essentially fuelling their external behaviour.

It is hard work to make sense of children's communication and respond appropriately to the signals sent to us. However, remaining open to this and attempting to connect with our children is important and helps them to meet their developmental milestones. By respecting a child's point of view, whether it's the same or different as our own, teaches them that they are trustworthy and that they can make good choices. Children feel secure and are more likely to behave in acceptable and considerate ways when their parents are able to set limits and provide appropriate boundaries. Remember that an angry and upset parent will be of limited help in calming down a distressed or angry child.

Building your bag of tricks

Children need their parents to be able to regulate their own emotions and thus to make appropriate responses to their child's behaviour. Children need to feel safe so that they can move away from their parent and explore the world, knowing that they can return for nurturing as needed. It is our job as parents to enjoy our children and to value our time with them rather than simply managing difficult behaviour.

BAG OF TRICKS

How acknowledgement can be made effective.

1. **Non-verbal communication.**
   When communicating with children your tone of voice, facial expressions, the way your body moves, your posture, positioning and proximity are all as important as your words. Listening to children and fully understanding what children are saying involves not only listening to their spoken words and the tone of voice but seeing and reading their facial expressions, gestures, movements, positioning and posture. Listen to your child's feelings with your whole body, get down to their level, look at their face and speak calmly.

2. **Awareness.**
   When we think about acknowledgement and its effectiveness, it is important to understand two key elements. The first part is when a parent expresses how they feel about something that their child did; for example, 'I felt so proud seeing you be so gentle with your sister'. The second is when children then internalise this acknowledgement and begin to praise themselves; for example, 'I'm really good at being gentle, especially with my sister'.

3. **More positive attention, less negative attention.**
   Think about the behaviours you want to see more of from your child and try to catch them doing these behaviours. If your child does not usually comply with your instructions straight away, acknowledge them any time you notice them moving towards this behaviour, for example, 'Great job, you started to pack away your toys.' Perhaps you see them pausing to 'draw breath' in their undesir-

able behaviour and can praise them for this, for example, 'Thank you for using a calm voice.' If your child gets easily frustrated, don't rush to solve their problems. Instead affirm that you have faith in their ability to find great solutions: 'You can solve this problem, I am happy to help you think of ways if you need my help.' You can also catch them solving problems and comment on this, for example:

'Wow! Look how well you figured out the next game to play.'

'Great job of deciding what clothes to wear today.'

4. **Make a list.**
   Write down some labelled acknowledgement statements that you could use to target the behaviours that you would like to see more of from your preschool-aged child.

5. **Practise acknowledging your child's feelings.**
   Children act out their feelings with their behaviour and need help to manage strong emotions. Acknowledging feelings is a powerful way of helping children to remain regulated. It also helps them to learn that strong feelings can be both felt and tolerated by you and them. Help them learn feeling words such as, tired, grumpy, cross, sad, joyful, lonely and excited. You can also help them notice where they feel their feelings in their body. Ask them, 'Where do you feel that inside?' Identify with your child the difference between 'I think' and 'I feel' and talk about their feelings and how they think others are feeling. Affirm that all feelings are okay.

6. **Useful mantras.**
   'I won't let you do that when you are out of control.'

   'When you're out of control I'll help you calm down.'

   'It's okay to be angry but it is not ok to hurt others.'

   'I can't hear you when you scream.'

   'I won't listen to you until you tell me in a calm voice.'

   'You never get what you want when you have a tantrum.'

   'I am not scared of your anger.'

Chapter 6

Giving Effective Instructions and Choices

One of the most common errors made by parents is in how they give instructions to their children. Typically, parents will issue an instruction and get no response. Then, apparently being ignored, they will repeat themselves in a variety of ways in order to get compliance. When the child continues to ignore them, the parent eventually becomes angry and raises their voice, which in turn negatively reinforces the behaviour. The child learns to only respond when their parent is angry and loud. This locks both parties into a negative escalation trap.

Parents who get into the habit of using requests or giving instructions to children worded in a question format ('Can you say good bye now?') are often frustrated and confused as to why their children don't listen. This is essentially because such phrases are non-committal and the child interprets the directive as a choice, which can be accepted or rejected as they wish. This means that the request or instruction is on the child's terms and when they don't do as required we in turn get angry.

When we give clear instructions, children are more likely to comply. Clear instructions imply that an action is required, for example:

- 'James, tonight I will read you two stories and then we will say goodnight.'
- 'It's time to pack up your toys now.'

Children learn to respond better when there is an expectation that they will act in accordance with what has been stated.

The typical escalation trap

Parent	Child	Parent request
1. The parent makes a request	The child is not interested and/or may not hear. The request is perceived as a disturbance and the child ignores or does not acknowledge the instruction.	'James, can you please put away your books?'
2. The parent repeats the request a second, third, fourth, and even fifth time. With each repetition, the request changes to pleading, bargaining, reasoning and threatening.	The child continues to ignore and pretends not to hear what is being requested. This habituation has occurred as they are so used to their parent talking in the background and have learnt to tune them out.	'James, are you listening to me?' 'Why aren't you being a good boy?' 'I'm getting fed up with waiting.' 'You had better do as you are told.' 'Those books are still all over the room, and it's about time you put them away!'
3. Parent gets angry and demands that the child comply or face a punishment.	The child may argue, talk back, complain, whine, or run away and sulk/cry.	Parent with raised voice: 'Put those books away!'
4. Parent loses their temper and pursues the issue, escalating their threats. At this point the parent is often emotional and distressed.	The child screams, cries, argues and throws a tantrum. Some children give in to this level of parental anger.	Parent shouting: 'Put those books away now! Do you want me to throw them all in the bin.'

Typical requests made

Parent's request	Child's response
'Can you…?'	'Umm, no. Since you asked.'
'Why don't you…?'	'Because I don't want to.'
'You should…'	'I'll think about it. No, I don't think I will.'
'Don't you think…?'	'No, actually…'
'Would you like…?'	'No thanks…'
'I don't think…'	'Really? But I think something different.'
'It would be nice…'	'I suppose it would. But I'm still not going to.'
'How about…?'	'No, it's okay.'
'I really wish you would…'	'That is nice to know.'
'Okay?'	'Maybe, but no. Since you asked.'

How to stop the escalation trap

To eliminate the escalation trap it is imperative that parents delete all requests and choice statements from their vocabulary when there is no choice to be made. For example, 'Would you like to sit at the table now?' is better expressed as 'It's time to come to the table now.' 'Would you like to get in the bath now?' is better expressed as 'It's time to get in the bath now.'

Parents need to help their child learn to respond immediately instead of only when there is screaming and yelling involved. Parents need to be in control and remain regulated. You have the right to expect certain instructions be followed and that your child does the deeds that need to be done in an appropriate and considerate manner. To do all this with conviction you need to maintain your role as the adult and your child's role as the child. It should not be the other way around. You need to listen to what your child says and make decisions that are fair and reasonable for your family, not decisions based on making the child happy. However, remember that children are more likely to accept a decision they do not like if they feel that you have listened and treated them fairly.

Elevating your child's position to one that is level with yours may make them like you for a moment, but it does both of you no favours in the long run. Wishy-washy phrases are the ladder on which your children climb to get to your level. It is much better to let them grow into the job.

Instructions need to be direct and clear; they must state what is expected in a certain situation. As much as possible instructions should tell your child what you want them to do, not what you do not want done. When situations are regularly conflictual it can help to use puppets to role play expectations, cooperation and consequences.

Rewarding cooperative behaviour with something enjoyable is effective, for example, 'When you are finished putting your toys away, then we'll…' Incorporating an incentive is usually beneficial in having children do what is asked of them, for example, 'Put the toys away quickly, so we can go to the park.'

Alternatively you can offer a choice statement and thereby avoid direct confrontation, such as, 'Will we get the blocks or all of the books first?' In so doing, parents give a children control and power in an appropriate way which does not reduce their in-charge position. Building fun into the instruction also helps with cooperation, such as, 'Put all the animals into the box and let's count how many animals we can pick up from the floor.' By building fun into the activity children are more likely to comply with the instruction and see it as a pleasurable connecting experience.

It is important that you give instructions for a new task once the child has completed the current one. Both you and they need to be focused when the instruction is given; for example, turn off the television before you ask your child to get their shoes. In that way, their focus is on you and what you are asking them to do rather than on the television.

It is important that the expectations of your child are developmentally appropriate and that they hear the instructions given. The best way to ensure that this happens is to get close to your child before speaking. Using your proximity and being an arm's length away ensures that they will hear what it is that you are requesting. Make sure that you give them enough time (five seconds) to process your instruction and to follow through. If they still don't alter their behaviour or follow your instruction, then logical consequences can be implemented.

If they ignore you or begin to demonstrate other challenging behaviour, you must act immediately. Giving warnings before the change of activity is one way to potentially avoid challenging behaviour. Using simple time methods works well such as: counting, songs, a short piece of music, using an egg timer or marking the time on a wall clock for preschoolers.

Simple steps for effective instruction giving

Step one

Use your proximity. Move closer and get to your child's level. An arm's length away is usually a good distance. It is also useful to use their name and make a connection with them.

Step two

Make sure that the instruction is to the point, clear and brief so that it is understood. For some children it helps to ask them to repeat the instruction and to acknowledge that they have understood: 'Yes, that's right.'

Step three

If there is a list of instructions, break them down and give them one at a time.

Step four

Make sure your instruction is the last thing that the child hears. If you need to explain anything, do this at the beginning; for example, 'It's time to go now. Stop playing and put your toys on the shelf now, thank you.'

Step five

Always use positive language when giving instructions; for example, 'Walk inside the house' rather than 'Don't run inside'.

Step six

Give your child time to cooperate (five seconds) and respond before you repeat the instruction.

Step seven

Avoid giving an instruction, leaving the room and then returning a period of time later to check.

Step eight

After giving an instruction stay focused on the task. Avoid distracting them from what you have asked them to do.

Step nine

Use labelled acknowledgement when your child follows an instruction. Describe exactly what they did well; for example, 'I felt so pleased to see you listening and getting quickly into your car seat, thank you.'

Step ten

When instructions are not followed issue a choice statement and follow this by a logical consequence; for example, 'You need to put your shoes on before you can go to the park.'

Terminating instructions

As a parent it is best to use terminating instructions when asking a child to stop doing something; such as, 'It is time for dinner. Put your toys away now, thank you.' In other cases, terminating instructions can be used to address inconsiderate behaviour:

- 'No. I can't let you hit me. We use our gentle touch.'
- 'No. Biting hurts. We don't bite people. Use your gentle touch.'

Step one

Immediacy is important. As soon as you notice challenging behaviour, stop what you are doing and gain your child's attention by saying their name and getting down to their level. Start by asking 'What is the rule about this?' or 'What happens if…?' At the same time acknowledge and affirm their feelings: 'You are really mad. What else can you do to use up your mad feelings?'

Step two

Clearly and firmly state what you want your child to do; for example, 'Sarah, you need to keep your hands to yourself, thank you.'

Step three

Use descriptive acknowledgement when you child does what you've asked; for example, 'Thanks for using your gentle touch.'

Step four

If your instruction is not followed, a logical consequence can be applied; for example, 'You are not playing gently, now the blocks will have to go away.'

Children quickly learn to cooperate when instructions are clear, respectful, firm and consistently delivered in a predictable manner. Appropriate consequences or giving choices are all about teaching children how to change and regulate their own behaviour. This will not occur overnight, but if you remain fair, firm, patient and consistent, you can avoid out-of-control arguments and damaging power struggles with your child.

Parents need to be respectfully in charge. When parents are in charge, they are aware of their child's needs, are able to set fair limits, and listen to their child's requests and questions.

When parents are clear, calm, consistent and assertively in charge, children feel safe and secure. As parents, we need to listen to our children while remaining firm and loving in our expectations of them and their behaviour.

The in-charge parent

The representation of the relationship between parent and child for an in-charge parent should be like this:

Not the other way around:

Remember, as parents we need to be thoughtful and courteous. After all, it is unreasonable to demand considerate behaviour from someone whom you do not always treat respectfully. You are your child's greatest teacher. The following formula is helpful when composing your instructions:

    [insert task here]
    + thank you

or

    [Child's name]
    + It is time to [insert task here]
    + thank you

It is straightforward and effective, as long as you are prepared to follow through with consequences in cases of unresponsiveness. See how much more 'in charge' you could sound while being polite and specific with your instructions.

Examples of specific instructions include:

- 'James don't throw toys.'
- 'You can throw balls outside, but you can't throw toys inside.'
- 'Don't hug hard it hurts, hug softly.'
- 'I want you to tell me in your big girl voice.'
- 'While I am talking to Mary you need to be quieter.'
- 'It's time to come to the table for dinner now, thanks.'
- 'Go back to bed.'
- 'It's sleep time, do you want your teddy or your dolly.'
- 'Speak using a calm voice, thank you.'
- 'Sam, stop or we will leave.'
- 'Touch baby very gently.'

Consequences work well when they are approached through choice. For example, after your child does not respond to an instruction to pack away their possessions you can say, 'Put this book on the shelf, I will help you, one thing at a time.' Without adding the supportive statement, 'I will help you', the task may seem overwhelming to your child, resulting in a refusal to comply with your request. However, it is vitally important that you are consistent and follow through with any stated consequence.

Implementing consequences isn't the only challenge; choosing them can also be difficult. When selecting a consequence, make sure that it is something that will work within your family, is realistic and can be followed through. Begin using consequences in one or two areas of your child's inconsiderate or problem behaviours. In this way you will not add unnecessary pressure by changing everything at once, and this will allow a smooth transition for your child into the new system. As you begin to follow through with consequences, you will notice that your child will start to follow instructions and will be better able to gain your attention in positive, rather than negative, ways.

Using choices with your child

Choices enable children to develop decision-making skills. Unless they are overwhelming, choices also help children develop their own personality. Choices allow children to evaluate things for themselves and to understand consequences through taking responsibility. They are important and assist children in developing their likes and dislikes and feeling as though they get a say in their own lives, even if it is only on a small scale. Making choices provide children with an opportunity for them to feel as though they are in control, and they are therefore more likely to comply, which will limit your frustration as a parent.

It is important that choices are limited to just two. It is also essential that parents are willing to accept the child's decision. In some cases, particularly with toddlers, the choice may be both. Effective use of choices include:

- 'Would you like a banana or apple?'
- 'Would you like to wear your blue jeans or red leggings?'
- 'While I do up your seat belt do you want to hold your bear or dolly?'

These sorts of statements allow your child to have choice and be powerful in a way that enables them to feel safe.

How to make instructions effective

Step one

Clearly state instructions in a calm and friendly manner. Remember not to make your instruction a question.

Step two

Give your instruction twice to start a behaviour and once to stop a behaviour.

Building your bag of tricks

This bag of tricks approach is aimed at reducing opportunities for damaging expressions of parent–child conflict and encouraging cooperative relationships within your family. The bigger your bag, the more likely you are to see the behaviours that you want to see and less of those that are unproductive. This approach will not only let your child know that you see when they are frustrated or angry but also show them effective ways to deal with these often intense feelings. Ultimately these strategies will assist you in setting reasonable limits and expectations and give you the skills that you need to respond quickly when limits are exceeded.

BAG OF TRICKS

1. **Choose an achievable goal.**
   Pick your most frustrating behavioural problem to concentrate on first. Don't try to change everything at once. Solve one issue before moving on to your next target behaviour.

2. **Be consistent.**
   As much as possible, all the adults who care for the children at home need to agree to use the same strategies in the same way and back each other up. This is crucial as mixed-up parenting encourages children to behave inconsiderately.

3. **Persist.**
   Select a few strategies from this book that you think will work for the target behaviour that you have chosen. Concentrate on putting your new ideas in place for at least one to two weeks before you move the goal posts or add different goals.

4. **Be kind to yourself.**
   For most parents, new strategies are hard work at first, but after a few weeks, they become habit. You won't really have to think about them too much, and you will be ready to add more tricks to your bag.

5. **Stay positive.**
   Change can take time. When you are learning anything new it can take two to four weeks for you to become comfortable with, and consistently, use the new strategies.

6. **Believe in your child.**
   Children can take two to six weeks to really learn their new way of functioning and for old habits to be replaced by more constructive and appropriate strategies for getting their needs met.

7. **Believe that change is possible.**
   Remember that although this book has lots of techniques, you know your child best, and you may have some good ideas of your own; only change what is not working!

8. **Take good care of yourself.**
   It is difficult for you to consistently meet your child's needs if you are neglecting your own. Try to create time to relax and do an activity that you really enjoy.

Chapter 7

Managing Parenting Challenges

Consequences

While development comes naturally to children, understanding behavioural expectations does not. Preschool-aged children are more able to develop an internalised ethic and to understand boundaries and expectations when they are consistent, clear and fair. As parents, we sometimes ask our children questions such as 'Why do you never listen to me?' This is often said as part of an attempt to understand why children act in certain ways, especially when their behaviour is challenging. It can sound like an accusation, inadvertently creating greater hostility in the relationship between parent and child. This sort of situation often comes about when a parent feels frustrated or angry and wants to ensure their child knows how bad they are feeling. This is a negative and unhelpful approach, which at worst can become abusive as anger and frustration increase.

'Why' questions are problematic. Children can rarely provide an answer and they may even respond by getting upset. This response does not ease the situation and often just intensifies your feelings. It also creates a situation where the child feels as though whatever they say or do will be interpreted as inadequate or wrong. A more effective way of addressing behaviours that you are not happy with is by using consequences.

Avoiding arguments

It is not possible to be an 'in charge' parent when you are dysregulated and arguing with your child. When you are feeling hurt, frustrated, or angry it may be difficult to stop yourself from engaging in an immature and destructive situation although this will not lead to resolution of the problem. When you do take part in arguments at your child's level, you open yourself up to being unable to model appropriate communication or address the problem in a constructive manner.

Reduce negative emotional expression

Shouting is the result of parental dysregulation and is often an approach used when people are frustrated or angry. It may work in the beginning but as time progresses children become accustomed to this strategy and tend to stop responding. This *habituation* tends to lead to an escalation with no long-term improvement in behaviour, or worse — cooperation only when the parent displays this level of aggression and loss of temper. The same occurs when smacking is used as a form of punishment or a strategy. These are not effective methods of parenting, as they do not form good long-term patterns of behaviour and often result in children becoming oppositional. A child will respond better if they view their parent as rational, calm, respectful and loving.

Another important factor in limiting the expression of negative emotions is to model respectful communication within the parental relationship. Children are unable to feel calm and safe when their parents are hostile towards each other. Parents need to act as role models so children can learn how to deal with conflict and behave appropriately. This behaviour will be projected on to other people in their life such as parents, peers and other adults. Modelling based on the example of highly conflicted parents often causes children problems in future relationships.

When children become aware of arguments within their home, they not only worry about the prospect of separation and having to choose sides, but may also feel that they are responsible for the conflict. All parents disagree from time to time and it is healthy for a child to know this, but they must see that you address any issues in a considerate way.

Planned ignoring

One of the most powerful techniques available to parents is the use of their attention. In general terms, pay extra attention to any behaviour you want to see repeated in your child and ignore negative behaviours. Many toddler behaviours disappear over time when parents withhold their attention. Ignoring essentially removes the reward for the child's negative behaviour. Obviously you cannot ignore dangerous or serious behaviour, but *planned ignoring* can be very effective for minor attention seeking behaviours. Behaviours such as nose picking, using rude words, refusing to eat, winging and whining all respond well to ignoring. This is particularly effective in the home environment where the parent is not pressured to take action and can respond decisively if the behaviour changes or escalates.

Planned ignoring works by withdrawing eye contact immediately and having no verbal or physical contact after an initial signal such as, 'I will talk to you when you are calm.' Parents should then not talk to the child until they stop the undesirable behaviour. Don't make a big show of this. Simply act as if the behaviour is not happening. However, it must be remembered that planned ignoring can lead to an initial escalation in the attention seeking behaviour before it wanes. This makes it an unsuitable strategy for behaviour that is likely to escalate and become dangerous to people or property such as running on the road, breaking things or playing roughly.

Give the child your full awareness immediately when the negative behaviour stops and make a positive comment that acknowledges the more desirable behaviour, such as, 'I like it when you ask for what you want in your normal voice'. Some parents prefer to signal their intention to ignore, for example, 'I cannot talk to you when you are screaming. You need to use a calm voice'. Further stating, 'When you stop screaming we can continue with our plans of… [something the child is eager to do]'. This strategy teaches children that they cannot get your attention by doing irritating and inconsiderate things. Instead they learn that acting in a reasonable and regulated way brings them your attention and positive feedback.

Logical consequences

Logical consequences should be short, immediate and respectful to the child's feelings. Over time children need to learn that consequences for undesirable behaviour are fair, appropriate, predictable, consistent and immediate. Logical consequences are not meant to be a punishment, but rather to teach. They are designed to give children the skills to be responsible for their own actions, to calm the situation, to discourage negative attention seeking behaviour and, as the child grows older, to make things right with others.

Logical consequences should be based around dealing with behaviour when it happens, rather than including all past events in the way that punishment often does. The implementation of logical consequences needs to be kind and firm and can be introduced as choices; for example, 'If you keep leaving the dinner table, I will think that you have finished eating and I will take your food away.' If you are consistent in the application of consequences, your child will learn to correct their own behaviour.

Consequences are about teaching children how to change and regulate their own behaviour; such as, 'When you are ready to be quiet in the car, I will continue to drive us to… [this is most powerful if you are going somewhere the child is interested in going]'. Consequences that limit parental attention and those that have a natural consequence to the behaviour are powerful for children in the early years. For example, throwing the toy out the window means it is gone, or playing roughly with a toy means it breaks. As children start to develop an understanding of cause and effect, time, and the relationship between their actions and consequences, they respond to consequences that have a deterrent value such as — no dessert, no play date or not being allowed to go to a birthday party.

Change in behaviour will not occur overnight, but if you remain firm, patient and consistent, you can avoid out-of-control arguments and damaging power struggles with your child. Below is a step-by-step guide for how to effectively use logical consequences.

Step one

Give your instruction in an effective way (as discussed previously).

Step two

If your instruction is ignored, follow through with a logical consequence even if it is inconvenient. It is important that the logical consequence matches the behavioural error; for example, 'Stop screaming or we will leave'.

Step three

Explain the consequence and do not argue the point.

Step four

Once the instruction has been followed, discuss with your child what should occur next time.

Step five

Repeat the logical consequence if the behaviour recurs and follow up with some *Quiet Time* if required.

The main aim of logical consequences is to teach children how to make good choices through experience. Consequences need to be kept consistent, fair, brief and realistic so that you can follow through with them, and your child can both learn and practise the correct behaviour.

Quiet time

Quiet time involves placing a child on the fringe of an activity for a short period of time if they start to demonstrate inconsiderate actions. It is not designed to be exclusionary but rather to allow them time to calm and regulate their own behaviour. The goal is to have the child re-join the activity as quickly as possible in order for them to then practise the considerate actions required to remain in the game.

Step one

Explain how quiet time works to your child. This may involve discussing what behaviour will result in quiet time and why you are using this as a consequence. This should also include a rehearsal of what will occur if quiet time is used.

Step two

When inconsiderate behaviour begins, gain the child's attention by stating their name and then firmly but calmly giving a terminating instruction; for example, 'Jesse, you need to keep your hands to yourself and use your words'. It is important that you act quickly when this sort of behaviour occurs.

Step three

If your child responds immediately then thank them and redirect their behaviour to a new task. If the behaviour continues or starts again within a short period of time, follow up the instruction with some quiet time. Clearly state what your child has done wrong and the consequences for their actions; for example, 'Sam, you are still yelling, so you now need to have some quiet time'. For children under three years of age this should be a very brief moment but can be more structured as they near their fourth year.

Step four (for children aged three and above)

Ask your child to sit on the fringe of the activity. The most effective quiet times are those that are short. Quiet time should not exceed half a minute for children under three and one to two minutes for children aged three to five years. Clearly explain the procedure of quiet time: 'Once you have sat here quietly for one minute, you may play with your sister again'. If your child continues to be disruptive, then a logical consequence needs to be applied. If they have escalated you will need to explain that they now need to be taken to 'cool down'.

Step five

Once your child has stayed quiet for the agreed period, you need to involve them in a new activity, without mentioning what has happened. You must also keep an eye out for positive behaviour; for example, if you see your child sharing their toys with their sister after they have been sent to quiet time for snatching, make sure you use descriptive acknowledgement to encourage them to continue this behaviour.

Cool down

Cool down is the next step of consequences if your child does not respond to your limit setting or when their behaviour has escalated to a point where they cannot respond to any direction or instruction. Cool down is a structured management tool designed to help children learn to manage their own behaviour and to calm down. It removes the child from any attention for a brief period and gives the parent a concrete management tool for behaviour that cannot be ignored.

Cool down is designed to interrupt the child in the midst of behaving inconsiderately, removing them to a designated spot. Then the parent completely removes their attention and remains bland, disinterested and temporarily unavailable. There should be no loss of face for the child and they should receive no attention when in cool down. The child is only allowed to leave cool down when they have calmed down.

Remember, children strive for parents' attention whether it is positive or negative. Removing your attention immediately when your child begins to behave in unacceptable ways is an extremely effective means of changing that particular behaviour.

The key with cool down is to be clear and consistent. The most powerful form of reinforcement is intermittent reinforcement. That is, if you respond to inconsiderate behaviour inconsistently, you can expect that particular behaviour to be more stubborn to eliminate. Your children will continually invite you to be consistent and offer you more opportunities to be consistent in your implementation of reinforcement and consequences.

Before getting started:
- Choose a cool down spot that lacks stimulation — the cool down spot should be a space for the child to actually cool

down. This could be a particular chair or step. It is a good idea to mark this out with a sticker to preclude arguments.
- Run through all the steps with your child before you implement this strategy.
- Make sure that you have a timer that can be used for older children.

The key to the effectiveness of cool down is in how quickly you act. The quicker you act the better the response. With time, cool down allows your child to understand that consequences increase if their behaviour does not improve or in fact gets worse. Cool down allows other family members to have some time to calm down too.

Young children may need their parent to sit close by and provide supportive statements such as:

- 'You're calming down now.'
- 'You need to breath slowly.
- 'When you're calm you can…'
- You can do this, calming down now…'

Step one
Give a clear and calm instruction without expressed anger; for example: 'Stop screaming, you need to calm down'.

Step two
Within five seconds, give a warning: 'This is your warning. You need to… [restate what you have just asked your child to do or stop doing].' Stay calm and do not add any extra instruction.

Step three
If your child does not respond within five to ten seconds, state: 'You need to go to cool down' in a firm but not angry voice.

From this point on, do not talk to your child or make eye contact, remain bland and disinterested.

Step four
Place your child in cool down. You may need to physically guide them to the cool down area.

Step five
Set the timer for preschool children from four years of age onwards. For children under three years of age half a minute is sufficient. It is generally accepted that one minute for every year from three to five years of age is best.

Step six
Allow your child to leave when the timer rings or, if they are under three years of age, when they have been settled for a few moments. If the child has not become settled you need to say in a bland tone of voice: 'You were not quiet/calm when the timer went off, so now you need to stay there until you have been quiet/calm for half a minute'. Reset the timer and walk away in a neutral calm manner. The goal is to not reinforce the disruptive behaviour.

Post-incident discussion
When cool down is over the parent changes from being bland and disinterested to warm and welcoming and needs to redirect the child into a new activity. When children move into the preschool years and have the language skills and an understanding of cause and effect, a post-incident discussion should occur. This is also an opportunity for a healing reconnection with their parent. This is possible by having a calm conversation about what happened and what could have been done differently. This allows your child to understand that

when they make mistakes they are able to make things right (to restore their relationship) and learn to take responsibility for their actions. It is vital that this discussion also offers acknowledgement for what they did well so as not to focus solely on the negative. For example, 'Once you went to the kitchen for cool down, you sat quietly and when you returned to the game we were playing, you waited your turn.' Such positive connecting experiences accumulate over time and it is through these moments of interactive repair that children are able to develop a sense of self.

Corrective feedback should be supportive and focus on the behaviour not the child. Say 'It is not okay to pull your sisters hair' rather than 'You are such a naughty bad girl.' By offering feedback at the time of the negative behaviour you give the child the opportunity and learning experience to associate the feedback with the behaviour. For example, 'I know that you felt angry, but hurting is not okay, we keep our hands and feet to ourselves.' When we acknowledge some positives children are able to internalise the idea that they are lovable but that their behaviour was not okay. For example, 'It was wrong to hurt your sister, but thank you for helping me to pack away the toys when I asked.'

Managing high-risk situations

Before the situation:

- When scheduling a trip or visit, try to organise it to fit in with current sleeping and eating habits of the child and general family.
- Make sure that you manage your time effectively so that any high-risk situation does not cause excessive stress or rushing. This is especially important when getting ready to go out.

- Explain to your child what is going on, whether it will be a quick trip to the shops, a few family members coming over for dinner, or a long drive or plane trip. Make sure you allow them to ask any questions they have and that you answer them.
- Discuss with your child what the consequences will be for considerate behaviour ('We will be able to stay longer') and for inconsiderate behaviour ('We will have to leave early').
- Agree on two or three engaging activities and prepare to implement these if your child gets bored or restless.

In the situation:

- Notice your child behaving considerately and acknowledge this behaviour.
- Watch out for boredom and be ready with alternative activities if needed. In situations such as when visitors come to lunch, make sure that you give your child attention now and again, and make sure you include them.
- When your child begins to behave inconsiderately, immediately gain their attention and redirect their behaviour.
- If the behaviour continues, give a firm but calm instruction and a reminder that the consequences discussed will be implemented if the considerate behaviour occurs ('We will be able to stay longer').
- If the inconsiderate behaviour continues, then follow through with the consequence discussed for inconsiderate behaviour ('We will have to leave early').
- Where possible, use your humour and even turn the situation into a game; for example, if you are cleaning up, you could say 'Okay let's see how quickly we can clean up'.

Calming strategies

When children are out of control, there is no use in stating consequences because they are out of their window of tolerance and therefore unable to respond. They cannot process what has been said. At these times children need assistance to regulate and calm.

Step one — remain calm

You cannot help your child to calm down when you are out of control.

Step two — label your child's behaviour

'Sarah you are out of control.'

Step three — go to your child and speak calmly

You may have to hold them, hug them, rock them, or quietly sing to them. Make statements that will help to regulate the child and to calm and de-escalate the situation:

- 'I am going to help you calm down.'
- 'I am not going to let go of you until you calm down.'
- 'I am not afraid of your anger. I love you and I am not going to let you hurt anyone.'

Step four — move your child away

If necessary, move your child away from the problem situation so that there is not an audience and so that your calming attempts are successful.

Step five — rest

After your child has calmed they are likely to be very tired and may need to rest or engage in a calm activity with you; for example, drawing, reading a book or going for a walk.

Even if your child is lacking self-control, you can still focus on considerate behaviour once they are calm. Have a follow up conversation with your child and ask 'What happened?' and 'What could we do differently next time?' You may need to plan ahead for the high-risk situation and/or modify the situation. Make sure that you end this process by reconnection and by acknowledging and affirming your child for what they did considerately and for calming down.

Building your bag of tricks

When we are consistent, clear and fair in our expectations we give our preschool-aged children a better chance to be able to develop an internalised ethic. Consequences, when applied from an in-charge position, allow children to feel safe and secure, assist in avoiding arguments and reduce negative emotional expression. The consequence should match the inconsiderate behaviour. Consequences can range from the simple to the complex: from the use of effective instructions or planned ignoring through to logical consequences, quiet time and cool down. The use of the calming strategy is appropriate when children are out of control, as there is no use in stating consequences when they are out of their window of tolerance and therefore unable to respond. As children get older post incident discussions should follow inconsiderate behaviour and any resultant consequence.

The following bag of tricks will assist you in positive long-lasting change in the interaction you have with your child. These will not have a noticeable effect immediately, but with time and commitment, the change will occur.

Behavioural strategies for children in the early years

BAG OF TRICKS

1. **Focus on effective instructions.**
   Say what your child CAN do, rather than what they can't. For example, 'You cannot ride your bike inside but you can ride it outside.'

2. **Have predictable and flexible routines.**
   These reduce the intensity and frequency of behavioural problems.

3. **Use Rituals.**
   Rituals such as stories before bed time or baths with Daddy each night or the same song before nap time or cuddles in bed in the morning, strengthen the parent-child relationship and help to repair relational rupture after conflict.

4. **Distraction is an effective strategy.**
   Distraction can be used for avoiding tantrums and redirecting children up until they are three years of age when their short-term memory is still developing.

5. **Use statements not questions.**
   For example: 'Let's see who is the fastest at packing away these toys' rather than 'Could you pack away these toys?' Asking a question often invites a 'no' response.

6. **Make good use of labelled acknowledgement.**
   This means telling the child exactly what you liked about their behaviour. Statements such as 'Great counting' or 'I loved the way you shared that toy with your sister' are examples of labelled acknowledgement. Contrary to some advice, you cannot acknowledge your child enough – particularly if it is labelled acknowledgement. Remember, the behaviour you acknowledge is more likely to be repeated by your child in the future.

7. **Use your proximity when giving instructions.**
   This means getting close to your child – no further than an arm's length away – and getting down to their level. You will be less likely to have to repeat instructions using this method and more likely to engage your child. In

addition, use your proximity as a barrier to pre-empt aggressive or disruptive behaviour.

8. **Use logical consequences.**
Consequences should be directly related to inconsiderate behaviour and administered as soon as possible after the event. By doing this, children learn what they have done wrong. For example, if children are fighting over a toy, prompt removal of the toy for a short period of time will help them learn their behaviour is unacceptable.
Likewise, if the child is using the toy in an aggressive manner, briefly explain why you are removing the toy and then remove the toy.

9. **Give children a small choice with some aspects of their life.**
For example, 'Would you like milk or water to drink?' This helps them feel empowered.

10. **Watch for triggers.**
Be aware of, and plan for triggers of possible disruptive behaviour for example, trips to the supermarket, car trips and tiredness. In this way you may be able to pre-empt negative behaviour and save you both a battle.

11. **Use 'attachment rich' and 'attachment neutral' parenting to manage positive child behaviour and inconsiderate behaviour respectively.**
Parents and children can get trapped in a cycle whereby the child develops more and more negative behaviours to attract the attention of a parent. This negative behaviour then becomes attachment rich, and is rewarded by the parent through more attention, albeit negative. Parent responses to positive child behaviour should aim to be attachment rich and responses to problem behaviour attachment neutral.

12. **Redirect behaviour before it gets out of control.**
This is particularly useful when, for example, you can see two children wanting to play with the same toy, or when a younger sibling wants to disrupt the activity of an older child. Redirecting can prevent rivalry between the children and promote pro-social turn taking and sharing.

13. **'Teach, don't punish' your child.**
Avoid the reinforcement trap – the more a child engages in undesirable behaviour, the less likely a parent is to

reinforce the child for positive behaviour. Teach and acknowledge desirable behaviour and you will be teaching your child the way you expect them to behave.

14. **You may want to consider using physical restraint to hold and contain a raging child.**
   This ensures both the child and you are safe. There are courses you can attend to learn to administer this method of restraint.

15. **Constantly demonstrate and reinforce considerate behaviour with your child.**
   Model using your words, compromise and empathy.

Chapter 8

Pulling it all Together — Your Bag of Tricks

When deciding what strategies to put into your bag of tricks, remember that you know your family situation inside out. By being clear in your goals for your family, you can make your parenting role easier. This bag of tricks approach is about not tolerating intolerable behaviour. Rather it is about positively guiding children's behaviour, giving them a sense of organisation and helping them to regulate by making their outside world predictable and controlled. When you show a child that you are on their side even when their behaviour is unacceptable, they learn what to expect from others, especially from parents and caregivers. Ultimately these tricks are designed to guide, as opposed to control, children and stem from the acknowledgement that children, by virtue of being children, will make behavioural errors. These powerful strategies appeal to children's pride, reason, logic and concern for others.

Your bag of tricks may include some or all of the following below.

Tips for encouraging considerate behaviour
- Consider your child's needs and respond to them when necessary.
- Spend time with your child individually, doing things that they like to do.

- Acknowledge their accomplishments and appropriate behaviour and minimise negative reinforcers.
- Cuddle, laugh and have fun with your child often.
- Listen and respond to your child when they ask for your help, information, or when they want to tell you something.
- A clear structure, particularly with regard to eating and sleep routines, is reassuring and helps children feel safe.
- Provide a good language model for your child (that is, avoid baby talk).
- Provide lots of interesting and stimulating books, toys, games and activities to encourage play, talking and intellectual challenges.
- Avoid situations that your child finds boring or uninteresting when they are tired or hungry.
- Model considerate behaviours that you want to encourage in your child (for example, helping others, being a good listener, using a pleasant voice, using gentle touch, taking care of your belongings, being friendly, cheerful and interested in others).
- Guide the family, rather than having either an 'anything goes' attitude or insisting on being the boss.
- Use natural consequences for considerate behaviour. For example, when a child says 'Thank you', instead of you saying 'Good girl', say 'You're welcome' or 'It's a pleasure' or give them a hug.
- Establish guidelines that define considerate behaviour. For example, the house expectation that everyone keeps their hands and feet to themselves. Guidelines help make your responses predictable over time and leave you free to decide how to respond, depending on the circumstances.
- Regard behavioural mistakes as natural — remember that thoughtless behaviour occurs because children are unable

to behave like adults, they have to learn how to behave considerately. It is your job as a parent to teach this complex skill to your child.
- Modify your demands. When children's actions indicate that they cannot cope, you can change what you expect of them.
- Adjust routines or change the environment to avoid inconsiderate behaviour when necessary — consistency is important, not rigidity.
- Allow children to do things themselves as often as possible.
- Support children to solve their problems when they are in conflict.
- Give children choices when choices can be made.
- Be wise in your decision-making. It is okay to be flexible and change your mind as long as you are not allowing intolerable behaviour.
- Teach self-control when children are out of control. Most children in a tantrum know how to behave but are temporarily overwhelmed by their feelings and cannot act on that information.

Have a stepladder of tricks in your bag, for example: humour, acknowledgement, effective instruction delivery, choice statements, logical consequences, quiet time and then cool down only when necessary. The strategy must be appropriate to the degree of inconsiderate and inappropriate behaviour and to your child's developmental capacity.

Tips for discouraging inconsiderate behaviour

- Anticipate likely problems and make the necessary adjustments. High risk times include: eating out, transitional times of the day or evening, shopping, long play dates and

your lack of availability such as when you are attending to emails/phone calls etc.
- Some behavioural problems can be avoided by simply changing expectations. For example, give finger food when faced with refusal to eat from a spoon, or feed a child at a small table when they insist on getting out of a high chair during meal times.
- Remain calm when speaking to a child who is upset or dys-regulated. Avoid becoming angry when your child is upset — speak calmly but firmly.
- Have realistic expectations.
- Get into the habit of telling your child what it is you would like them to do rather than not do.
- Tell children that it is their behaviour that you do not like, for example, 'I don't like *it* when you…' rather than, 'I don't like *you* when you….'.
- Ensure you gain your child's attention and give them thoughtful attention when you are speaking to them.
- Use short sentences when issuing instructions.
- Issue choices and be willing to accept your child's decision.
- Avoid vague acknowledgement such as, 'good girl' and give concrete messages and clear instructions.
- Give plenty of notice before activities change.
- When asking the child to perform a particular behaviour stay with them and watch them to ensure follow-through.
- Children in the early years do not generally hurt others on purpose and need to learn what 'gently' means.
- Respond to inconsiderate behaviour immediately, consistently and decisively.

- Set limits to your child's behaviour. Do not give in and accidentally reinforce or encourage your child for being inconsiderate (for example, when they demand or whine).
- Respond to inconsiderate behaviour by telling your child what to do as opposed to what not to do (for example, say 'Use a calm voice', rather than, 'Stop yelling'). Try to avoid unclear instructions or requests (for example, 'don't be silly').
- Back up your instructions by using choice statements, natural or logical consequences, quiet time and cool down.
- Prevent problems by ensuring that your child has plenty of interesting and engaging things to do.
- Remember, during the preschool years children are not good at sharing. Help them get ready to share, for example, by letting the child pass the cake or other special things.
- Keep a look out for when your child is behaving considerately and make sure you acknowledge it — expectations can be linked to a personal quality, such as 'I saw you…; that was really helpful'.
- Remember, to choose your battles — focus on your target behaviour(s).
- Children's feelings should always be acknowledged, especially when they are upset, anxious, angry or frustrated.
- In a situation where a child makes a behavioural error and acts inconsiderately, it is important to acknowledge the child's feelings, explain the boundaries in regards to the situation and reiterate what the considerate behaviour is for the situation. Verbal responses should be as brief as possible.
- Consistency is vital — children will push poorly defined boundaries. If you are finding it difficult to be consistent with the expectations that you have set, then you may need to review them. Sometimes difficulties arise because an expectation is too restrictive, not age or developmentally

appropriate or a child does not have the physical or intellectual capabilities to comply with the expectation. Keep your expectations reasonable and persist. It may be challenging in the beginning, but you will find that your parenting role gets easier.
- Immediacy in giving acknowledgement and consequences is key to their effectiveness.
- Only give directions or instructions that you are prepared to follow through.
- Issue effective instructions; for example, go to your child and state their name rather than yelling an instruction from across the room.
- Be specific with instructions so that there is little room for misunderstanding; for example, instead of saying 'go away', if you need the child to leave the kitchen as you are cooking at the stove and it is hot, you should say, 'it is not safe to play games in the kitchen. Go and play in the lounge room, thank you'. While in the short term, all of these additions to giving an instruction may be tiring, it will result in a positive long-term effect of establishing healthy habits in your child in regards to listening and following instructions.

Children during the early years experience a similar range of behavioural problems. Although there is no magic solution the information contained in these pages is a general guide and offers strategies that usually work. By having realistic expectations of yourself and your child, by considering their developmental level, by trying to see things from your child's point of view, and by looking for the reasons behind inconsiderate behaviour, parents are more able to feel resourced in their parenting.

As a parent, it is important that we steer away from threatening, nagging, shouting, verbal aggression and humiliating behaviour directed at children. While we all are aware of the need to do this, we can find ourselves slipping into these patterns when we are feeling stressed, tired, angry, or frustrated and it's unrealistic to expect you'll get things right all the time. Nevertheless, if you take the ideas outlined in this book and build your skills over time, you will find that the moments of frustration and exhaustion become less and less.

You are your child's greatest resource. Following the recommendations and suggestions in this book will help you to develop considerate, sensible and independent young people. Reaching out and asking for support and help if needed is a sign of strength and takes courage. Seeking support reflects the love of your child, your insight that there is a problem, your desire for things in your family to be different and your commitment to working towards a harmonious home environment. Ultimately your relationship with your child will be nurtured and you will be able to experience more of the joy and richness our children bring to our lives.

Regardless of our own parenting experiences we can strive to be the best parent we can be. This book is aimed to be a bag-of-tricks approach to assist you in your parenting role in raising happy, well-adjusted, confident, considerate and independent children during the formative years of their life. The ideas contained in this book are designed to provide the foundations to help your child achieve their potential socially, emotionally and intellectually now and in their development into their adult self.

Parenting tips

Tip one — be consistent

By being consistent, your child knows what they are expected to do and what happens if they behave inconsiderately.

Tip two — making promises

If you make promises, be careful to ensure they are something you can keep. Sometimes you will need to change your decisions on certain things but make sure that you explain the reasons for change to your child.

Tip three — consequences

Punishment is unwise. Use consequences. Consequences must not be humiliating, they should relate to the inconsiderate behaviour and should be followed through with as soon as possible. The withdrawal or limiting of affection should never be used.

Tip four — follow through

Mean what you say and act on it. Threats of consequences are not nearly as effective as following through with a discussed consequence. Remember, children learn best from experiencing something themselves.

Tip five — expectations

Ensure that the expectations you have for your child's behaviour are reasonable for their age and capability.

Tip six — acknowledgement

Ensure that you acknowledge considerate behaviour when it occurs more frequently instead of just implementing consequences when inconsiderate actions occur.

Tip seven — apologise

If you are in the wrong or have behaved inconsiderately apologise and let your child know that you were wrong and it was not their fault. Children in the early years are very forgiving and love us no matter what. When we model respectful communication and a willingness to apologise children learn to do the same.

Tip eight — be a role model

Practise what you preach. Children in the early years imitate what they see. By being treated with respect and dignity they will in turn treat others well.

Know your parenting strategy

Children in the early years need to feel safe, secure, loved, and to know that their parents and caring adults will have clear expectations, make fair requests and set appropriate limits on their behaviour. Parenting children in the early years is hard work. It challenges our competence, energy and emotions. Parenting challenges our ability to establish firm, consistent, clear, predictable, and yet loving boundaries.

Being intentional and planned in the parenting strategies that we use, in the ways we make parenting decisions and how flexible we are in our actions, allows for kind, empathetic, assertive and compassionate parenting. Such mindful parenting allows children to develop self-knowledge and an ability to have autonomous ethics or what can be termed considerate behaviour which develops throughout the early years.

The development of considerate behaviour and a spacious window of tolerance can be greatly assisted by the parenting strategies utilised in this book. A bag of tricks approach to parenting in which the relationship is built on respectful practice with the goal of teaching children rather than controlling them facilitates autonomous ethics. Mindful parenting grounded in the assumption that children are hardwired to change and adapt allows us as parents and caregiving adults teach and guide children's considerate behaviour and their development of autonomous ethics. During the early years behavioural techniques aimed at building considerate behaviour are useful and can be used to direct both considerate and inconsiderate behaviour.

References

Illsley Clark, J, Davenport, G, Grevstad, M, Hansen, S, Houtz, N, Kemp, S, Lawrence, M, Montz, D, Nordeman, G, Paananen, M, Peterson, E, Popp, J, Salts, J & Weiss, M (1994). *Help! For Parents of Children from Birth to Five.* Australia: Harper Collins.

Illsley Clark, J & Dawson, C (1998). *Growing Up Again 2nd Edn.* Minnesota: Hazelden.

Kabat Zinn (1994). *Wherever you go, there you are.* London: Piatkus Books.

Schore, AN (2003). Affect Dysregulation and Disorders of the Self. New York: Norton.

Stern, D (1985). *The Interpersonal World of the Infant.* New York: Basic Books.

www.ingramcontent.com/pod-product-compliance
Lightning Source LLC
Chambersburg PA
CBHW051756230426
43670CB00012B/2314